DATE DUE

AP 20 '98			
AP 21 '98			
AP 1 ? 0?			
AP 17 '07			

#47-0108 Peel Off Pressure Sensitive

ALLIANCES
AND AMERICAN
FOREIGN POLICY

ROBERT E. OSGOOD

THE JOHNS HOPKINS PRESS
BALTIMORE AND LONDON

To
Clara A. Anderson
and the memory of
James K. Anderson

PREFACE

This book manifests the continuing interest of the Washington Center of Foreign Policy Research in alliances, represented in *Alliance Policy in the Cold War,* edited by Arnold Wolfers (1959), and *Nations in Alliance,* by George Liska (1962). In the literature of political science, alliances—with the exception of particular alliances, like NATO—are, surprisingly, quite underrepresented, considering their importance. This effort to illuminate the subject originated in a group study conducted by the Center for the United States government. It is essentially an expansion and revision of my own contribution to that study, borrowing freely but highly selectively from my colleagues.

The other contributors were John C. Dreier, William C. Johnstone, George Liska, Charles Burton Marshall, Vernon McKay, Robert W. Tucker, and Arnold Wolfers—all permanent faculty members of The Johns Hopkins University or associates of the Center or both; Seyom Brown, then on leave from RAND Corporation and serving as Research Associate at the Center and Visiting Lecturer at the School of Advanced International Studies; and Walter C. Clemens, Jr., then Assistant Professor at Massachusetts Institute of Technology. I am indebted to them, but they are not responsible for the use I have made of their works.

I greatly appreciate the meticulous and penetrating reading of the manuscript by Fritz G. A. Kraemer, Research Associate of the Center, on leave from the Department of Defense. I also wish to thank Charles R. Planck and P. Edward Haley for their research assistance. I am particularly grateful to Naomi Schwiesow, who, in addition to research assistance, provided invaluable help in matters of substance and form at all stages of the manuscript and devised the index. I am indebted to Elaine Clark for her expert supervision and execution of the secretarial work.

Washington, D.C.   Robert E. Osgood, Director
October, 1967   The Washington Center of
                                    Foreign Policy Research

CONTENTS

ix

ALLIANCES AND AMERICAN FOREIGN POLICY

CHAPTER

I

ALLIANCES IN THE COLD WAR: VISION AND REALITY

1. *The Thwarted Ideal*

The tremendous extension of American commitments since World War II seemed imperative to the nation because it was directed at countering communism, a totalitarian ideology with pretensions to global revolution that confronted the United States with a dual threat, to its security and its international ideals.[1] This threat was assessed in the light of the lessons of the interwar period, which seemed to warn that it was necessary to check totalitarian expansion by stopping the first steps of piecemeal aggression against the "free world" in order to avoid a chain of aggressions leading to another world war. This assessment of the communist menace in terms of fascist expansionism inspired a tremendous concentration of American energy and power abroad, comparable to the energy mobilized in the two World Wars.

In America's sustained effort to prevent the extension of communist control, alliances have played an especially important part. Not only have they been a major means of projecting American power; they have also been the most prominent instrumentality by which the nation has related

1. By American commitments I mean all the government's foreign pledges, undertakings, and contracts that establish some expectation or obligation that the United States will use its military power—overtly or by threat—or help other countries to use theirs for specific purposes.

1

itself to a vastly expanded role in the international arena. In addition to being calculated instruments of deterrence, alliances have appealed to the American ideal of organizing order by means of collective institutions. They have been the nearest thing to "collective security" in a world of power politics.[2] They have been documentary evidence of America's effort to organize the "free world" against "communist aggression." Thus, in hundreds of pronouncements, official and unofficial American spokesmen have hailed the forty-two allies of the United States as interdependent links in a collective system of deterrence, which departs from old-fashioned alliances and provides a barrier against the anarchy of nationalism. Secretary of State Dulles spoke of "the free-world network of collective security," a "nearly world-wide system of regional collective security [which] has . . . deterred aggression."[3] "The integrity of these alliances," said Secretary of State Dean Rusk, "is at the heart of the maintenance of peace, and, if it should be discovered that the pledge of the United States is meaningless, the structure of peace would crumble, and we would be well on our way to a terrible catastrophe."[4]

In the American vision of international order, multilateral "regional" alliances have a special place because they presumably transcend and subordinate separate national interests, represent indigenous harmony and initiative, and permit the United States to be one among several "partners," even if it is the senior partner.[5] The American ideal of regional alliances is enshrined in the United Nations

2. See pp. 17–18, 44–45.

3. *Department of State Bulletin*, no. 986, May 19, 1958, and no. 954, October 7, 1957.

4. Address to the United States Chamber of Commerce on May 1, 1967.

5. See, for example, the statements about "a world of regional partnerships" by President Johnson and by the President's Special Assistant, Walt Rostow, in the *Department of State Bulletin*, no. 1422, September 26, 1966, and no. 1464, July 17, 1967.

Charter as part of a compromise between the competing concepts of regional and universal methods of organizing world peace and security.[6] The ultimate expression of this ideal would be a kind of world concert of more or less self-sustaining regional organizations for external defense and internal security. Each would combine the highest functions of NATO and the Organization of American States (OAS) but have purely indigenous leadership, and each would take care of the peculiar problems of its own region while retaining harmonious ties with the others and, of course, with the United States in particular. In a sense, this is the Wilsonian ideal of national self-determination adapted to the new imperatives of international co-operation.

But ever since the extension of American alliances beyond Europe, the vision of a global network of alliances has grown dimmer. The problems and limitations of existing alliances have become more conspicuous. Only in NATO has there been anything like a collective defense effort, and there the problem of eliciting military co-operation has become more and more frustrating, while the defection of France has called into question the viability of the whole institutional superstructure. As issues of diplomacy and interallied politics supersede the problems of deterrence and defense, the psychological burden and political liability of maintaining American military preponderance in Europe, seemingly for an indefinite period, grows heavier.

Yet no other alliance approaches the working collaboration that NATO exhibits, since none rests on anything like

6. With the existence of mutual assistance pacts like the Anglo-Soviet pact of 1942 in mind, Article 53, while normally requiring prior authorization of the Security Council for "enforcement action" under "regional arrangements," waived that requirement with respect to measures taken against a renewal of aggression by former enemy states. With the evolving American regional system in mind, Article 51 recognized the right of states to exercise individual and collective self-defense "until the Security Council has taken the measures necessary to maintain international peace and security."

as solid a political capacity for effective co-operation. At the same time, American alliances, taken as a group, do not constitute even a loosely knit *system* of alliances. Each reflects a distinctly different set of interests with little relation to other alliances. They are interdependent only in the sense that American power, the common denominator and indispensable core, is at stake in each. Furthermore, far from approaching self-sufficiency, all are to some degree vehicles of American military preponderance so far as their external security functions are concerned. Actually, all of the alliances account for only a fraction of the commitments of the United States in the vast areas outside the Western Hemisphere and Europe. As its commitments have expanded and the cohesion of its alliances has diminished, the United States has felt less need for, and seen less prospect of, obtaining prior agreement from its allies before using, or even deciding how to use, its armed forces.

Alliances are nevertheless a very important part of current international politics generally and of American foreign policy in particular. They will remain important because they are bound to be an integral feature of political life among interacting sovereign states. The question is how their quantity, form, substance, and functions will be affected by basic changes in the international environment and what their role will be in relation to the role of other kinds of commitments. Because alliances, from the American standpoint, have played such a prominent part in the cold war, the most important issues of American policy are entangled with the future of alliances. As the most binding and far-reaching kind of obligation between states, alliances are at stake in the anxious question raised by the war in Vietnam, as it has been raised in the case of every other critical foreign involvement since World War II: Are American commitments exceeding American power?

2. The Problem of Preponderance

At the root of this question is the psychological and political problem of America's military preponderance in most parts of the world. America's problem is not simply how to keep its commitments commensurate with its material power. America's present commitments are well within its military capability if the nation is willing to expend enough of its material and moral energy to support them. Even where the support of commitments seems to require intervention in a partly civil war in support of an ineffectual government, as in Vietnam, the United States can at least prevent a communist victory if it is willing to pay the price indefinitely. The problem of American preponderance is rooted in a sense of disproportion between the nation's conception of its interests and the price it must pay to support them. As the nation discovers the bitter consequences of pursuing an over-all objective virtually identical with the containment of communist expansion, this sense of disproportion raises two profound questions: What are the vital interests of the United States; that is, what interests are worth supporting militarily at the cost that must be paid? And how can the United States support the whole range of its interests as effectively as possible, with a level of effort and involvement that the political will and genius of the nation can sustain?[7] The problem of preponderance becomes especially acute as foreign involvements divert attention and resources from domestic crises.

The severity of this problem is perhaps exaggerated by the

7. This study does not examine the validity of the prevailing American consensus about national goals and interests or evaluate the current criticism of this consensus. Rather, it aims to show the consequences of this consensus for the role of alliances in American policy. I do assume, however, that the existing consensus is quite likely to continue to prevail, barring a traumatic military defeat in Vietnam or elsewhere combined with a very severe domestic crisis.

wave of criticism and anguish stirred up by the war in Vietnam, which is singularly unpopular and difficult to resolve. It is also exaggerated by the defenders of American policy who evoke an image of a beleaguered United States, virtually alone in containing the relentless pressure of Soviet power, the fanatical stirrings of the Chinese colossus, and a tide of communist revolutionary aggression. Nevertheless, even without these wartime exaggerations, there would be a serious conflict between the apparent requirements of supporting America's global interests and the nation's willingness to pay the cost.

The attainment of unrivaled world-wide power by the United States and the corresponding expansion of its view of American interests have been accompanied by a vast extension of American commitments which shows no signs of coming to a halt. In the course of attaining this global position, the United States has formed more alliances, engaged in more military interventions, and undertaken more foreign expenditures and other involvements than all the other states put together. Yet, despite the pressures that impel great states and empires to conserve their power and protect their commitments in the face of adversity, the United States has little taste for the glories and agonies of preponderance. If its power is in a sense imperial though not imperialistic,[8] it has acquired its "empire" not as a result of an acquisitive or missionary spirit but because it has resolutely carried out the logical consequences of a conviction that American security and welfare—and, coincidentally, the prospects of a better world—depend upon the containment of communist expansion. Nevertheless, having attained an "empire," it finds an overriding concern, which is even broader than the containment of communist expansion, in the promotion of an international order that is as safe and as congenial as possible for the United States, with its vast power and commitments, to live in. Under these circumstances Americans

8. See George Liska, *Imperial America: The International Politics of Primacy* (Baltimore: Johns Hopkins Press, 1967).

will face a psychological and political problem of preponderance as long as there are powerful forces in the world, communist or otherwise, that threaten to disrupt the territorial status quo, upset balances of power, and generate wars—and this seems likely to be the situation for a very long time.

The burdens of American preponderance can be mitigated, perhaps, by more discriminating policies, but the determining conditions of preponderance are largely beyond American control, given the nation's conception of its world role. One crucial condition is simply the absence of other major states with sufficient power and sufficiently convergent interests to supplant or complement American power in fostering an international environment compatible with America's basic objectives. The pervasiveness of this condition is indicated by its existence even in Western Europe, where one might suppose that the political and military prerequisites of self-defense are abundantly present.

Most Americans would agree that, ideally, the United States should look forward to a time when its European allies would organize collective power by themselves so that they could defend themselves independently and exercise greater independent political weight in the world. This is not only because such European collaboration would relieve the military and economic burdens of the United States, but also because, in the long run, the United States is apt to find it much more difficult and less satisfactory, even if feasible, to elicit the consent or acquiescence of dependent states than to harmonize American policies with the policies of states that are able to act on their own initiative. (This assumes, of course, a basic convergence of vital interests in both cases.) For the United States, the problem of dealing with strong and self-reliant nations is in the end less onerous, and more edifying, than the problem of dealing with weak and eventually frustrated or demoralized dependents. Dependence seldom elicits proportionate co-operation, and preponderance seldom provides commensurate control. Indeed, the luxury of assured protection encourages a freedom of maneuver and an irresponsibility on the part of the protected that is denied the protector. States most immediately affected by a threat to their security, even if they do not perceive that threat exactly the way the United States does, are usually in a better position, politically and psychologically, to cope with it. Moreover, although it is more difficult in some ways for the United States to pursue deterrence and other ends by accommodating its policies to those of other great powers, the existence of such powers would tend to give it greater room for error without disastrous consequences by reducing the risk that its own decisions will be absolutely determining and their consequences irrevocable.

In reality, however, even the nations of Western Europe, which have a capability to manage their own military and political destinies that is unapproached by any other group of nations, remain largely dependent on American military power. Two decades after a war from which they have long since recovered economically, they show few signs of fulfilling the original postwar expectation that they would assume the major burden of their own defense in return for an American guarantee. Nor have they satisfied the abiding aspiration of an influential group of "Europeanists," in the United States as well as in Europe, that they should federate and deal with the United States as an equal partner in the Atlantic Community. Consequently, the United States has remained in the unenviable position of continually twisting the arms of its allies to do things for their own welfare that they would be quite capable of doing for themselves if they would concert their efforts.

If there are substantial reasons that even the European members of NATO remain virtual dependents of the United States in the management of the military balance, there is little likelihood that other states will be less dependent. The burdens of preponderance in Europe may nevertheless decrease *if* the Soviet military threat remains minimal and *if* a revival of independent political activity in

Europe does not pose new and acute problems of order and security. Elsewhere, however, the burdens of preponderance are likely to increase, for there are no other groups of states that approach the Western European states' political and cultural affinities, basic identity of interests, mutual trust, and capacity or inclination for dependable co-operation with the United States.

In the next decade, regardless of the outcome of the Vietnamese war, the United States may face the problem of promoting a balance of power in Asia to protect surrounding states against Chinese pressure. Even if China were to become destitute and fragmented, a surrounding balance of power would be necessary to prevent a recurrence of the old problem of imperial rivalries in a new form. If the United States is the only major noncommunist supporter of equilibrium and order in Asia, it is bound to confront a far more difficult and uncongenial task than it has encountered in Europe. Just maintaining the credibility of its present commitments and preserving the cohesion and security of its existing alliances in Asia will be difficult enough, as local nationalism asserts itself and as China's nuclear power grows. For example, a restless but militarily impotent and dependent Japan might be a much greater political burden on the United States than West Germany has been.

If the United States continues to adhere to containment in the face of threats to the security of noncommunist states on the Eurasian periphery and to oppose violent changes in the status quo by unfriendly forces, how can it avoid the maintenance, and even the extension, of its military preponderance throughout much of the noncommunist world under increasingly disadvantageous conditions?

One way to mitigate this tendency would be for the United States to exercise greater selectivity in the application of containment by military means. It might, for example, make more effort to distinguish prospective areas of communist penetration that can and must be defended from those that are unsuitable for American military counterintervention because the local states are not sufficiently viable or do not have sufficient intrinsic value. The United States would then count on the intractability of unstable situations to hostile control, on the competition between the Soviet Union and China, on the independence of other communist states and parties, and on local nationalism to discourage communist seizure. There are trends in this direction. The Vietnam war, whatever its outcome, is likely to make the United States more cautious about becoming involved militarily in internal wars. If Indonesia continues to reject communist influence internally and externally, the United States may be less apprehensive that regimes not adjacent to China or North Vietnam need its military intervention to avoid subversion. Of course, there are some areas that do not enjoy Indonesia's geographical insulation and that are likely to be vulnerable to communist subversion in the absence of an American commitment to their defense. And the peculiar conditions that may enable communist regimes to pursue an independent course like Yugoslavia's are too rare and problematic to rely upon. Nevertheless, the special political and military conditions that enable North Vietnam to penetrate South Vietnam and even withstand a massive American intervention exist nowhere else in Asia.

Another way to mitigate the burdens of preponderance would be to pursue an arrangement common in the history of imperial competition—the establishment of spheres of influence in which the United States, the Soviet Union, and China would grant each other paramountcy and freedom from intervention. For example, the United States has in effect recognized Eastern Europe as a Soviet sphere of influence. But what areas not now under communist control is the United States willing to write off as zones of unopposed Soviet or Chinese expansion? And what zones of communist nonintervention are the Soviets or Chinese willing to grant the United States reciprocally?

It would be more realistic, perhaps, for the United States to seek the establishment of zones of mutual nonintervention or at least of limited intervention. In effect, substantial areas of the world—for example, much of Africa—presently fall into this category because of the difficulty that any external power would have in gaining access to them or exercising control in them, because of the limited value of the stakes, and because of the tacit recognition that intense competition for control would raise the level of effort and enhance local leverage without producing a commensurate pay-off. But where these conditions do not exist, nonalignment by itself carries no assurance of the limitation or exclusion of external intervention; areas that are in contention, like Laos, cannot be effectively "neutralized" without fairly active American intervention and a credible military presence in the background to maintain the local balance of power.

3. A Pluralistic World

In any case, we must prudently anticipate that there will continue to be a few important areas, especially areas within the shadow of China, where communist or other hostile pressure is active and cannot be contained merely by local resources without the help of outside countervailing power that goes beyond economic and technical assistance. In these areas the only hypothetically effective defense other than an extension of American military power, whether projected by means of alliance or otherwise, would be indigenous centers of power. Considering the magnitude of Soviet and Chinese power, such regional and local countervailing forces would have to be based on a combination of power among several states. To establish such a combination where none has existed would probably require an alliance. Hence, the establishment of counterpoises to the Soviet Union and China that do not require American preponderance may depend on the creation of local or regional alliances.

Even if Soviet restraint and Chinese weakness made such counterpoises unnecessary, the United States, by virtue of its global power position and the local demands upon it, would have a general interest in there being a reasonably well-structured pattern of international relations to restrain local imperialism and provide indigenous states with a measure of autonomy and invulnerability against external intervention. For this purpose too, local non-American alliances might serve American interests well. Without them, local balances of power, like that in the Near East, might have to be maintained artificially by external military assistance, creating all the political difficulties for the United States that such an expedient would entail. The United States might or might not be the guarantor of such alliances. It might (as in the case of CENTO) provide them with military assistance and co-operation without taking the role of a hegemonic member.

In Africa, for example, a network of parallel or countervailing alliances, related to ex-metropoles or other advanced states, might constitute the most satisfactory link possible between the less developed countries and the mainstream of international politics, supplementing the link provided by the United Nations. As a form of embryonic order for the less-developed states, indigenous alliances might be preferable to grand designs of regional or continental unity. Such designs are apt to be so unrelated to reality as to reduce small states to posing on the international stage and recording votes in a kind of facsimile politics that is largely irrelevant to real national conflicts.

But the fact is that the capacity of the economically (and, in general, politically) underdeveloped states to establish self-regulating systems of alliances and to sustain stable balances of power has not been demonstrated, and it is doubtful that it will be for an indefinite period. Therefore, the most promising alternative to an expanding American global preponderance may be a world of five or six superpowers, all mutually restrained and all confined to moderate ambitions by the inherent constraints of a multipolar international system, with each superpower assuming a burden of alignment and alliance appropriate to its special interests and the scope of its effective hegemony.[9] This is an attractive vision in many ways, appealing to America's ideal of harmonious, self-reliant regionalism and promising a more agreeable division of labor in the world, yet preserving a major role for the United States as the most powerful state. But is this vision realistic? Is a united Western Europe, Japan, India, or even China likely to play the envisioned role of superpower? Would such a "regional" world really be stable and peaceful? Would it be congenial with American interests?

Americans have dreamed of escaping the burdens of preponderance through the emergence of a pluralistic world in which progressively more interdependent states in homogeneous regions would be largely responsible for their own defense. But the dreamers have overestimated the feasibility of several centers of power, galvanized into a community of free states by their common opposition to an aggressive bloc that threatens the security of all, and led by the persuasion and example of the United States. If a more pluralistic world is really emerging, it is likely to be much less neatly

9. This grand design is elucidated in Roger Masters, *The Nation Is Burdened* (New York: Alfred A. Knopf, 1967), especially pp. 108ff. For an earlier exposition of the multipolar ideal, in which, however, the emergence of powerful industrial states in the presently underdeveloped areas was anticipated, see Walt W. Rostow, *The United States in the World Arena* (New York: Harper and Brothers, 1960), bk. V, pt. II. Rostow wrote, "It is, therefore, as sure as anything can be that the central international problem for the future is the organization of a world community in which the United States, Western Europe, Japan, and Russia are joined by powerful industrial states in Asia, Latin America, the Middle East, and Africa—in about that order; and that, within something like seventy-five years, the bulk of the presently underdeveloped areas will have attained economic maturity" (p. 413).

organized and much more intractable to American influence than this, although it would not necessarily be a world of international anarchy and war.

In the next decade or so international politics is likely to become considerably more pluralistic, as measured by the emergence of new centers of diplomatic influence and, perhaps in Asia, even of independent military power. This trend offers the prospect of the United States supporting its basic interests on a less ambitious scale of commitment and responsibility, if only because other states will have a greater role to play in determining the balances of military and political power. But the price of such a mitigation of preponderance will be the sacrifice of direct control and influence, as in the relationship of protector to dependent, for more indirect methods. The United States will have to make up for its reduced opportunity for direct leadership by opportunistic maneuvering in an increasingly variegated and fluid field of power and interests. Instead of trying to organize the "free world" against "international communism," it will have to expend its energy in promoting, through selective support, inducements, threats, and sanctions, a more complex balance of power in which the distinctions between foe and friend break down into numerous gradations along a broad spectrum of conflict and alignment.

In this kind of world one would expect alliances to continue to play a vital role in American foreign policy, but their role would bear little resemblance to the role they played during the onset of the cold war and the consolidation of containment. In the more complicated pattern of international politics that we must expect in the future, alliances, though in some cases essential, will be subjectively less satisfying and objectively less satisfactory as a medium for projecting American power and supporting American commitments across the oceans.

With these broad concerns in mind, let us examine in the following pages some of the primary factors and trends that are likely to affect the role of alliances in international politics in the next decade or two. Then we can consider their implications for American interests and policies.

CHAPTER

II

THE NATURE OF ALLIANCES

1. Why Alliances?

Alliances are an integral part of international politics. They are one of the primary means by which states seek the co-operation of other states in order to enhance their power to protect and advance their interests. This instrument of co-operation is so pervasive that every state must have an alliance policy, even if its purpose is only to avoid alliances.

The subject of this analysis, however, is broader than alliances. Alliances are only one kind of commitment by which states enhance their power. Moreover, there are many kinds of alliances, and alliances serve a variety of purposes. One cannot properly assess the value and the prospects of alliances without examining the alternatives to alliances and distinguishing between the various kinds of alliances.

In this study an alliance is defined as a formal agreement that pledges states to co-operate in using their military resources against a specific state or states and usually obligates one or more of the signatories to use force, or to consider (unilaterally or in consultation with allies) the use of force, in specified circumstances. It differs in principle from a "collective security" agreement. Strictly speaking, such an agreement obligates its members to abstain from recourse to violence against one another and to participate collectively in suppressing the unlawful use of force by any member. It may also obligate its members to resist aggression by a non-member against any of them, but what distinguishes it from a mere collective defense agreement is that it presupposes a general interest on the part of all its members in opposing aggression by any of them and entails procedures for the peaceful settlement of disputes among the members.

A defensive alliance presupposes only a common interest in opposing threats from specific states or groups outside the alliance and does not necessarily or usually entail provisions for settling disputes among its members. An offensive alliance aims at forcibly changing the international status quo, territorially or otherwise, to increase the assets of its members.

A defensive alliance may also be a local or regional collective security agreement. The OAS, for example, is both. Alliances, although ostensibly or actually directed against an external threat, may additionally or even primarily be intended to restrain a member, limit its options, support its government against an internal threat, or control its foreign policy in some fashion. In this respect, many alliances have actually been as much concerned as a collective security agreement would be with organizing relations between allies, although national sensitivities may have counseled against making such concern explicit or public. The internal concern of alliances tends to increase with their duration and with the diminished perception of an external threat.

Alliances commonly reflect more than a single, explicit, and identical interest between members. Allies may wish to support a variety of interests that include merely complementary or parallel interests and even divergent ones. Some of these interests may be specified in the agreement, but some are more prudently left unspecified, whether they are mutual or not. In any case, the full substance and significance of an alliance is seldom revealed in the formal contract or treaty for military co-operation, any more than the essence of marriage is revealed in the marriage certificate. The contract is simply an attempt to make more precise and binding a particular obligation or relationship between states, which is part of a continually changing network of interests and sentiments. An alliance, therefore, reflects a latent war community, based on general co-operation that goes beyond formal provisions and that the signatories must continually cultivate in order to preserve mutual confidence in each other's fidelity to specified obligations.

As a formal contract for military co-operation, however, an alliance may be difficult to distinguish from other kinds of military contracts such as military subsidies, military assistance agreements, or military base agreements. Most alliances specify (if only in a general phrase) the contingencies under which force will or will not be used by the members and against whom it will be used, but they may be worded so broadly that these particulars can only be inferred. Conversely, other kinds of military contracts may contain explicit political provisions concerning the use of weapons and facilities. In any case, like alliances, they are based on definite understandings and expectations (whether shared by both partners or not) about the purposes and circumstances of the specified military co-operation.

Even in the absence of formal contracts for military co-operation, unilateral declarations of intentions can go far to commit states to the use of force in behalf of other states. Such declarations are particularly important now that the communication of military intentions for the sake of deterrence plays such a prominent role in international politics. Their importance is indicated by their extensive use to reinforce and refine formal reciprocal commitments.

But military commitments need not depend even on unilateral declarations. They are often established and conveyed indirectly by countless official and unofficial words and actions, creating understandings and expectations that are no less significant for being implicit. These understandings and expectations are the substance of alignments of power and interest, and alliances and other explicit commitments would be useless without them.

Why, then, do states make alliances? Generally, because alliances are the most binding obligations they can make to stabilize the configurations of power that affect their vital interests. Alliances add precision and specificity to informal or tacit alignments.

More than that, the fact that alliances are *reciprocal* and *formal* agreements increases the obligation of signatories to carry out specified commitments and co-operation. The ceremony and solemnity accompanying the formation of an alliance signify that sovereign states have surrendered important aspects of their freedom of action and obligated themselves to an interdependent relationship.

Moreover, the obligation of alliance relates directly to the response of signatories to contingencies that call for a possible resort to war. Alliances impinge more fundamentally upon the vital interests of nations and more broadly upon the whole range of their foreign policies than agreements designed merely to provide for the use of goods and facilities. For this reason alliances are also more likely to provoke rivals and adversaries and lead to countervailing combinations, which may further limit the political options and enhance the interdependence of allies.

The political significance of alliances is all the greater in this era of popular (including undemocratic) governments because alliances generally presuppose national or ideological affinities that go beyond the matter-of-fact expediencies involved in more restricted contracts.

Thus, whatever its benefits, an alliance tends to cost more than other kinds of military commitments because it limits a member's political options and freedom of action more. For this reason the signatories of an alliance feel entitled to continual assurance of each other's fidelity and their own net benefit. Consequently, an alliance of some duration encourages further claims upon its members and tends to require repeated regeneration through adjustments of their liabilities and assets. Lacking recourse to supranational instrumentalities to enforce an obligation that could involve their very survival as nations, states must rely on diplomatic co-operation against an adversary and on other manifestations of good faith and common interest. These by-products of alliance may entangle states in each other's affairs to an extent that is not always easy to anticipate when an alliance is formed. As an investment in future returns of national security and welfare, an alliance is apt to be more open-ended and consequential than other kinds of military contracts. Therefore, although alliances are a pervasive element of international politics, the capacity and incentive for states to engage in alliance are far from universal. Relatively few states have the resources, the internal cohesion, or the coherence of national interests to become effective allies. Some states that will freely seek and accept military assistance or base agreements may regard even the most limited alliance as an unwise political entanglement.

2. The Functions of Alliances

There are four principal functions of alliances, and they are not necessarily mutually exclusive: accretion of external power, internal security, restraint of allies, and international order.

The accretion of power entails increasing the military power of allies by combining resources and eliciting positive co-operation. This has been the basic and the most common function of alliances. The ultimate purpose of accretion is to enhance the relative power of one or more allies against another state or states for defensive or offensive ends (although some states, especially the smaller ones, may want power largely in the form of status).

Internal security is sometimes a more important function of alliance for a weak state than accretion of its external power. In recognition of the international significance of internal threats and developments, which are often supported covertly from outside, alliances may be intended principally to enhance the security or stability of an ally's government or regime, often by legitimizing material assistance or military intervention against internal opposition. This purpose is usually not made explicit, however, since intervention in the domestic affairs of another state, even at that state's invitation, has acquired a stigma in the age of popular national governments.

Next to accretion, the most prominent function of alliances has been to restrain and control allies, particularly in order to safeguard one ally against actions of another that might endanger its security or otherwise jeopardize its interests. This function may be accomplished directly by pledges of nonintervention or by other reassurances that one ally will not contravene the interests of another, or it may be the by-product of commitments that limit an ally's freedom of action and provide its partner with access to, and influence upon, its government.

International order is the broadest and the least attainable function of an alliance. An alliance may aim to preserve harmony among its members and establish an international order—that is, a stable, predictable, and safe pattern of international politics—within an area of common concern. In its ultimate form, this function of an alliance becomes collective security. In different ways, the Quadruple Alliance after the Napoleonic Wars and the OAS have exercised this function of maintaining order. Before the onset of the cold war, the United States expected the Big Three, as the core of the United Nations, to be guarantors of a new world order. Some people believe that NATO has served indirectly as a framework for a new Western European order or even an Atlantic Community.

3. The Determinants of Alliances

Among the numerous factors that may affect the creation, continuation, or decline of alliances in various parts of the world, several "determinants" (in the nondeterministic sense) seem particularly important. These determinants also affect the characteristics of alliances and the nature of their functions, but they are principally relevant to the elementary questions of the existence or nonexistence, utility or disutility, and vitality or impotence of alliances. They are:

The pattern of conflicting and converging interests. If states have no interests that they need to support by military power against other states, they lack sufficient incentives to form alliances. If two or more states feel no need for each other's assistance in improving their military capacity to protect or advance their interests against other states, an alliance is not likely to be created, and an existing alliance is likely to erode.

Even if mutual military needs exist, the creation or maintenance of an alliance often requires a convergence of interests that goes beyond a common interest in security. Most notably, there must be sufficient affinity and harmony of policies. The importance of this convergence is directly proportionate to the comprehensiveness and mutuality of the alliance's obligations and to the duration of the alliance; it is inversely proportionate to the intensity of the security threat.

In the case of existing or prospective alliances in which interallied control or order is an important function, the urgency of a commonly felt threat to security may be less determinative, but then the pattern of conflicting as well as converging interests among allies becomes crucial.

The distribution of military power. The formation and preservation of an alliance depends on the military capacity of states as well as their political incentive to co-operate militarily (even though one state may only provide bases and facilities or promise to remain neutral). The capacity of states to help each other depends on the relationship of their concerted power to the power of potential adversaries.

The interaction of this distribution of power with the pattern of interests among states affects not only the desirability and feasibility of alliances but also the characteristics of alliances and the nature of alliance policies. For example, it establishes the polarity of power, or, more specifically, the number of states that are engaged in a dominant international political conflict, are projecting decisive military power, and are undertaking independent military commitments. Whether there are two, or many, "poles of power," has many implications for alliances, some of which we shall be considering.[1]

The changing distribution of power between an alliance and its opponents may affect the cohesion of an alliance. For example, adverse changes in the external distribution of power may create dissatisfaction with the distribution within an alliance. Such dissatisfaction and the effort to overcome it may change alliance policies and even alliance functions.

Alliance capability. Even if the preceding determinants should support the creation or maintenance of an alliance, the states that are concerned may lack certain minimum military and political prerequisites of alliance. Most important among these prerequisites are: (a) enough internal stability, executive authority, and economic strength, along with a sufficiently coherent and predictable foreign policy, to enable a state to be a reliable collaborator and (b) adequate capacity of a state to dispose its military power effectively for the benefit of an ally. (Again, the capacity of one state may be confined to a relatively passive role.)

Alliance-mindedness. Related to the preceding determinant, and also of special significance for the future of alliances among the small and newer states in the Third World, is the subjective attitude of governments toward alliances. For example, some small, recently independent states are averse to alliances with the chief protagonists of the cold war. The subjective inclination or disinclination to enter

1. Reference to poles of power may involve an awkward geometrical analogy, but common use of the concepts of bipolarity and multipolarity in discussions of international politics has nevertheless established this analogy.

alliances may be closely related to considerations of expediency; yet it goes beyond sheer reasoned calculation of security requirements and reflects hopes, suspicions, and ideals that are deeply rooted in the national culture and experience. In America's period of physical invulnerability and political insulation, its high-principled denigration of alliances was as important as its glorification of them in the cold war. These determinants should be considered as a whole because they reinforce, qualify, or offset each other. None of them is sufficient by itself to account for the past, present, or future of alliances. The first two determinants, however, are particularly important.

4. *The Evolution of Alliances*

All the functions and determinants of alliances that I have cited apply to contemporary alliances, but the context and methods of application have changed throughout modern history as basic changes occurred in the military and political environment. One way of comprehending these changes is to note the shifts of emphasis among several contrasting types of alliances: between offensive (or revisionist) and defensive (or status quo), wartime and peacetime, bilateral and multilateral, guarantee and mutual assistance, institutionalized and noninstitutionalized alliances. The distinctions among them should be apparent in the brief description of the evolution of alliances that follows.

In the eighteenth century, alliances were the primary means by which states tried to improve their military positions, since the strength of their armed forces was relatively fixed. The typical alliance was a bilateral agreement, or several interlocking bilateral agreements, made during a war or in anticipation of war, after which it was terminated or became inoperative. It usually involved one or several of the following kinds of commitments: a subsidy to support another state's troops; a guarantee to fight on the side of

another state (often with a specific number of troops) under
stated circumstances; a pledge of nonintervention or mutual
abstention from war in the event that one or both of the
signatories should become engaged in war with other states;
or a division of the territorial and other spoils of war.

Before the last part of the nineteenth century, alliances
entailed no extensive military preparations or co-ordination.
The undeveloped state of technology, the limited economic
capacity of states to carry on war, and the small scale of
warfare made such arrangements infeasible and unnecessary.
Moreover, states had few of the inhibitions against going to
war that arose later when modern war revealed its awesome
potential for civil destruction, and they lacked the need and
the capacity to sustain alliances as peacetime instruments of
military deterrence. War was not yet so terrifying as to create this need and capacity. It was a more or less normal
recourse.

Consequently, although there were a few multilateral defensive alliances of long duration, there were scores of offensive alliances—chiefly bilateral—that were intended to
acquire territory by means of war. Both offensive and defensive alliances aimed as often at restraining an ally by limiting his political options and deflecting him from an
opposing alliance as they did at aggregating military power.
The ideal was to keep alliances flexible and commitments
limited. Toward this end secret alliances and secret clauses
in published alliances were commonly arranged, not only to
conceal aggressive designs, but also to increase diplomatic
options by making deals with other states without giving
offense to allies.

The eighteenth and the first half of the nineteenth centuries were notable for the large number of alliances that
were formed and unformed; but a more significant feature
of alliances at that time was their limited and flexible nature, which enabled them to adjust readily to shifting interests with little regard for the later constraints of sentiment

and ideology or the imperatives of aggregating power in peacetime. The flexibility and secrecy of alliances created a good deal of diplomatic turmoil, but, because there was a fairly equal division of power among the several major states of Europe, these qualities helped to sustain a working equilibrium that restrained and moderated ambitions and acquisitions and kept any single state or coalition of states from dominating the others. The politics of alliances were punctuated by frequent wars, but the limited scale and destructiveness of warfare made it a tolerable instrument for maintaining an equilibrium.

The Napoleonic Wars revealed the new scope, intensity, and dynamism that war could attain when based on the mobilization of manpower and popular enthusiasm. This revelation compelled the European states to combine in a grand coalition to defeat Napoleon's bid for hegemony, just as they had combined against Louis XIV and earlier aspirants to hegemony. This time, however, a wartime alliance became a novel peacetime coalition. In 1815 the victors formed the Concert of Europe, which combined the eighteenth century conception of equilibrium (insofar as the territorial-political settlements and the Quadruple Alliance were aimed at checking France) with the new conception of a multilateral combination of states pledged to concert their power and to consult among themselves in order to preserve the international order against further liberal and nationalist revolutions as well as against divisions among themselves. Therefore the Concert might be called the first modern experiment to form an organization for international order—a forerunner of the League of Nations and the United Nations.

The Concert of Europe was undermined by differing national interests, especially by Britain's refusal to join in suppressing revolutions. After 1822, when the British left the Quadruple Alliance, nothing remained of the Concert except the habit of consultation during crises. International politics returned to flexible, limited, and mostly offensive alliances in a multipolar international system. Taking advantage of the fragmented structure of power, Bismarck acquired territory at the expense of Denmark and Austria, and he rounded out Germany's boundaries with a quick victory over France in 1871. He shored up his accomplishments with a complicated network of bilateral and trilateral alliances designed to keep power fragmented and to prevent combinations that could revise the status quo by setting up balanced antagonisms. Primarily his alliances were intended to limit the options of allies while keeping Germany's commitments to them equally limited.

Yet Bismarck actually helped to undermine his own system of alliances and to set the stage for a different kind of alliance system. The suddenness and decisiveness of Prussia's victories demonstrated the efficacy of its continuing peacetime military preparations, particularly the conscription system, the use of railroads, and the professional planning and direction of war under a general staff. To withstand such an assault, a state would have to be as well-prepared during peacetime as during wartime. Furthermore, military preparedness would require advance arrangements for the co-operation of other states and the co-ordination of military plans and operations. (The French defeat was partly due to France's mistaken calculation that she could acquire allies after war broke out.) The dramatic development in the last quarter of the nineteenth century of the technological and economic capacity of major states to advance their military positions by quantitative and qualitative arms increases indicated that the internal development of military capacity might replace shifting alliances as the dynamic element of power.

In these circumstances Bismarck's alliance system led to counteralliances that, under the growing pressure of military preparedness through arms races, tended to polarize international conflict between two opposing coalitions, the Triple

Alliance and the Triple Entente. These two alliances were far from being tightly knit diplomatically, and they were only partially co-ordinated militarily by military conventions and staff conversations. Nevertheless, they provided the political frameworks within which military commitments were consolidated; and the consolidation of military commitments in turn tightened the alliances. Thus alliances evolved from a means of fragmenting military power to a means of aggregating it.

The consolidation of defensive alliances before World War I, combined with the build-up of military power, made states more susceptible to being triggered into war by an ally (as Austria's war against Serbia entangled Germany). This consolidation encouraged a chain reaction of involvement, once war began, and practically guaranteed that any war involving one ally would become a general war. Nevertheless, if states had been primarily concerned with military deterrence rather than simply with preparing to fight, and if they had not permitted military plans (especially those for total mobilization) to take precedence over diplomatic opportunities to accommodate disputes short of war, the polarization of alliances need not have been incompatible with the peace and security of all. In fact these were not primarily deterrent alliances but rather alliances formed in anticipation of war. Unfortunately, statesmen deferred to their general staffs, who were absorbed in preparing maximum offensive striking power for a war that they expected to be as short and decisive as the Franco-Prussian War.

Contrary to prevailing expectations, World War I turned out to be a devastating war of attrition, and modern firepower chewed up the manpower and resources of Europe. This grim surprise led to a widespread reaction in the victorious countries against alliances, which were regarded as one of the principal causes of the war. Woodrow Wilson caught the popular imagination by proposing an "association" of power, in opposition to the discredited balance of power system. According to his conception of the League of Nations, all states would be organized against aggression from any quarter. He expected the chief deterrent to aggression to be the power of world opinion rather than the threat of force. Other American proponents of the League idea thought the United States should concert its power with that of Britain and France to preserve a new postwar order. However, it is doubtful that the nation as a whole was prepared to participate in power politics to the extent required of a major ally, for Americans still retained the sense of physical security that underlay their isolationist tradition. Until they became convinced by America's involvement in World War II and the onset of the cold war that aggression abroad impinged directly upon American security, they would not enter a peacetime alliance.

The ascent of Hitler's Germany showed that a peacetime deterrent coalition, whatever its effects in other circumstances might be, was essential to peace and order in the face of the most dangerous bid for hegemony since Napoleon. Unfortunately, the major democratic countries failed to form such a coalition. Although Wilsonian collective security would have been unworkable as a universal supranational order, even if the United States had joined the League, this ideal served as an excuse for avoiding an alliance, especially for Britain, which turned down France's bid for a defensive alliance against Germany. Yet World War II led the major democratic states to draw a lesson from this interwar experience that became the psychological foundation of America's postwar system of deterrent alliances. This system came to dominate the postwar history of alliances.

In the cold war, alliances have been as important in international politics as in any other period of history. But among the advanced states several developments have reduced their flexibility (but, by the same token, enhanced their stability). Their primarily deterrent function, the inhibitions against major states going to war in the nuclear age, the increased importance of peacetime military forces, the sensitivity of governments to public sentiment and ideological positions, the persistence of a dominant international conflict and structure of power that have been essentially bipolar—all these developments have tended to restrict the number of alliances and the frequency of shifts of alliance among major states. At the same time, the emergence of many new states in previously colonial and politically inactive areas has meant that the great majority of states lack the basic external and internal prerequisites for engaging in alliances. One consequence of these new constraints on alliances is that other forms of military commitments have come to play a proportionately greater role in international politics. Another is that intra-alliance functions have assumed greater importance. I shall examine these phenomena in the next three chapters on developments in the cold war and, in the final chapter, inquire whether there are factors that may further change the role and characteristics of alliances in the future.

CHAPTER

III

THE BEGINNINGS OF AMERICAN ALLIANCE POLICY

1. *The Onset of the Cold War*

In the cold war, when the United States became an active participant in *Realpolitik* for the sake of its own security, it reversed its historic rejection of alliances and embraced them as a deterrent to Soviet expansion. Because deterrent alliances were obviously defensive and public, and because the United States was more and more clearly the leader of the noncommunist states, alliances lost their stigma in American eyes and gained the aura of an instrument of international order. Multilateral alliances were the most attractive kind because they seemed democratic and representative. An institutionalized multilateral alliance was especially in accord with American ideals because it appealed to the principle of international co-operation that overcomes national divisions by means of formal organization. But the transformation of American policy toward alliances was not immediate; it developed only when there were major changes in the cold war and in America's conception of its security interests.

At the end of World War II the United States once more became the leading exponent of an international security system transcending the classic system of countervailing alliances. This time it supported the concept of a concert of great powers to make the system of collective security work. The United Nations would administer a postwar territorial-political settlement, provide for peaceful change, and oppose violent threats to the status quo. But the power of the United Nations was to reside in the Big Three (the United States, Britain, and the U.S.S.R.), which later (with the addition of France and Nationalist China) became the Big Five, or the permanent members of the Security Council. As a system for international security, the United Nations would be run by the concert of great powers, but its sanctions would not be applicable against these powers. Since each of the Big Five had a veto in the Council, the operation of the concert presupposed unanimity among its members.

In practice, however, the three principal members of the concert had quite different ideas about the substance of this condominium. The continuation of Anglo-American military collaboration perpetuated on a tacit and partial basis the war-born alliance, despite Washington's termination of the Roosevelt-Churchill agreement of 1943 to use the atomic bomb only by "mutual consent." But, even after the Czecho-slovakian coup of 1948, major differences between American and British interests and conceptions of postwar order precluded genuine alliance. Soviet interests were not only different; increasingly, they seemed deeply antagonistic. The gradual discovery that Russia was fundamentally an expansionist power (if only because it could not feel secure as long as its ideological opponents "encircled" it) and not just a traditional state trying to secure its territory by means of an Eastern European buffer, destroyed the projected tripartite arrangement before it actually operated.

Stalin was now cast in the role of a kind of Byzantine Hitler, pursuing hegemony with more circumspection but no less determination. Yet in the aftermath of the second world war in a quarter-century, and at the dawn of the nuclear age, war seemed too terrible to fight. Russia had to be checked short of war. In the absence of a working collective security system or a concert of power, military deterrence was the only method of establishing a restraining counterpoise, and the United States, despite its hasty postwar demobilization, had the most impressive means of deterrence—nuclear weapons.

Nevertheless, the United States was still sufficiently wedded to the traditional view of its detached role in the world to be reluctant to become the leader of a general deterrent effort, even in behalf of Western Europe, let alone other parts of the world. In entering the United Nations it had continued to eschew commitments to specific states. As the only member of the Big Three without such commitments, it envisaged its role as that of an impartial proponent of international order, mediating between the British and the Russians. Therefore, no less significant for the postwar pattern of alliances than the realization that Russia was an antagonist and not a collaborator, was the gradual discovery that the United States was the only power with the economic strength, the military potential, and the political will to deter Russia. The real beginning of this discovery came with the Greek civil war and Britain's withdrawal from primary responsibility for maintaining the integrity of its traditional sphere of influence in Greece and Turkey. America's new role was signalized by the Truman Doctrine and the Greek-Turkish Aid Program.

The Truman Doctrine, declaring that "it must be the policy of the United States to support free peoples who are resisting attempted subjugation by armed minorities or by outside pressures," was the first explicit official recognition by the American government of its role as an active participant in power politics. Yet the full implications of the Doctrine were obscure because it was open-ended and provided no explicit limitations, means, or priorities to indicate the extent of commitments and actions that the United States might undertake in carrying it out. Whether assistance to *free* peoples or opposition to communist aggression against *any* noncommunist nation was to be emphasized, the Doctrine was an expansive definition of American security interests—a bold projection of wartime aims into the cold war. But apart from aims, what means were envisioned, and, particularly, what was the role of military power to be? The answer to that question would determine the magnitude of America's global role, but that answer was ambiguous.

The juxtaposition of the Doctrine with what was in part a military assistance program to Greece and Turkey foreshadowed, if only indirectly, an extension of American military commitments. Yet, indicating the government's reluctance to face that prospect publicly (and also indicating a difference of opinion within the government about the Doctrine's military implications), President Truman added, "I believe that our help should be primarily through economic and financial aid which is essential to economic stability and orderly political processes." Despite this emphasis on nonmilitary measures, observers like George Kennan and Walter Lippmann saw in the Doctrine the seeds of an undiscriminating global engagement of American power. Yet Kennan's own seminal contribution to the new definition of American policy might legitimately be interpreted in an almost equally expansive fashion.

In a memorandum submitted in February, 1946, Kennan set forth propositions that were, in effect, the intellectual foundation of the Truman Doctrine. Later this was elaborated and published as an article, "The Sources of Soviet Conduct," in the July, 1947, issue of *Foreign Affairs*. Essentially he postulated—correctly, as subsequent events proved— that the Soviet Union, despite its unceasing concern to fill "every nook and cranny available to it in the basin of world power," could be deterred from expanding its area of control by the "vigilant application of counterforce at a series of constantly shifting geographical and political points" and that eventually the containment of Russia would "force upon the Kremlin a far greater degree of moderation and circumspection."[1] But precisely when, where, and how should the United States apply counterforce? Only unforeseen developments could answer that question.

Given the weakness and vulnerability of most of the noncommunist world in the face of Soviet and, later, Communist Chinese pressure, we can see in retrospect that it was virtually inevitable that the Truman Doctrine, backed by the theory of containment, should lead to a considerable extension of American commitments. Yet few imagined the range of these commitments at the time. Given the historic indispensability of countervailing military power as a restraint upon powerful states that, like Russia, were determined to change the political and territorial status quo, it seems to have been equally inevitable that American *military* power would be the primary element of containment. Yet the precise admixture of military power with other means of containment and the exact methods of deploying and organizing military power have been highly controversial from the beginning.[2] So the assumption by the United

1. More questionable was Kennan's judgment that the Soviet political system bore the seeds of its own decay and that containment would "promote tendencies which must eventually find their outlet in either the break-up or the gradual mellowing of Soviet power." The anticipated break-up has not materialized. Whether the frustration of Soviet expansionist tendencies has led to the permanent "mellowing" of Soviet power, as opposed to a transitory, tactical relaxation of pressure, remains to be seen. In any case, Kennan and most American officials were primarily concerned with the alteration of Soviet external behavior rather than with the liberalization or break-up of its internal political system, and they did not regard the latter as a prerequisite of the former.

2. A significant illustration of this point is that Kennan always disagreed with the American government's emphasis upon the military component of containment and preferred to stress political, economic, and even spiritual power. To him the Marshall Plan was the ideal means of containment. He was alarmed by the open-ended nature of the military commitment implied in the Truman Doctrine. He objected to the size of the military aid slated for Greece and opposed any aid to Turkey.

States of the task of containing communist expansion does not, in itself, account for the large role of alliances in American foreign policy.

The Truman Doctrine, contrary to some alarms at the time, was at the outset no more than a sweeping justification of a local response confined primarily to economic and political measures. The Marshall Plan, which followed immediately, extended the area of containment's application but kept similar restrictions on the means of carrying it out. At that time the United States had no alliance commitments outside the Western Hemisphere.

2. The Organization of American States

The commitment of the United States within the Western Hemisphere, which was given definitive form in the 1947 Inter-American Treaty of Reciprocal Assistance (Rio Treaty), did not grow out of the emerging conflict with the Soviet Union. Instead, the Rio Treaty grew out of experience with the Axis during World War II, and it developed naturally from the Pan-American system before the war. It was the latest in a series of moves, dating back to the 1920's, that were taken in order to give multilateral form to a commitment that traditionally had been undertaken by the United States unilaterally. In making this multilateral hemispheric commitment to nonintervention and consultation, the United States finally and formally accepted restrictions on its freedom of action that it had been in the process of accepting for almost three decades. The Rio Treaty and the 1948 Bogotá Charter of the OAS completed this process and established a regional security system, consistent with Article 52 of the United Nations Charter, which permitted "regional arrangements." Being restricted to the Western Hemisphere and consolidating an evolving hemispheric policy, the obligations of pacific settlement and of collective defense stipulated in these treaties hardly represented a new departure for the United States.

The OAS is based on an internally as well as externally oriented collective security alliance, since the Rio Treaty contains provisions for settling intrahemispheric conflicts peacefully as well as for collectively opposing extrahemispheric threats of aggression.[3] Yet the peacekeeping functions of the OAS have been invoked on only a few occasions in two decades, to prevent or pacify conflicts among Latin-American states. Not until the Cuban missile crisis were the sections dealing with an outside threat utilized (although Article 6 was invoked during the Guatemalan Revolution in 1954, then dropped after the collapse of the rebels). Only in the Dominican uprising of 1965 were OAS forces actually employed, being added to the controlling American forces after the crisis had been brought under control.[4] Although exposed states like Venezuela, Bolivia, and Guatemala have

3. Article 2 pledges the signatories "to submit every controversy which may arise between them to methods of peaceful settlement and to endeavor to settle any such controversy among themselves by means of the procedures in force in the Inter-American System before referring it to the General Assembly or the Security Council of the United Nations." Article 7 provides that "In the case of a conflict between two or more American States . . . the High Contracting Parties, meeting in consultation shall call upon the contending States to suspend hostilities and restore matters to the *status quo ante bellum*. . . ." Article 3 pledges the signatories to regard an attack from a non-American state upon one as an attack upon all and to consult about collective measures. Article 6 provides for consultation on collective measures "if the inviolability or the integrity of the territory or the sovereignty or political independence of any American State should be affected by an aggression which is not an armed attack or by an extra-continental or intra-continental conflict, or by any other fact or situation that might endanger the peace of America."

4. During the Cuban crisis, on the OAS Council's recommendation that members offer individual and collective measures against Soviet intervention, Argentina and the Dominican Republic sent naval forces, which were integrated with United States forces in a "combined quarantine force." Strictly speaking, therefore, this was a multinational force established by the states directly rather than a force under OAS authority, as in the Dominican crisis.

shown increasing interest in gaining OAS help against guerrillas from Cuba, the chief function of the organization in Latin-American eyes is not to suppress armed conflicts or aggression but rather to regularize relations with the United States in such a way as to impose constraints on the use of American power while maintaining a claim on its support if needed.

In practice, forcible intervention in the hemisphere against extrahemispheric aggression, whether direct or indirect, depends on the United States. It may try to get the sanction and co-operation of the OAS, but it will not necessarily make its action contingent upon OAS support. Without American initiative the OAS has neither the institutions, the political cohesion, nor the military capability to act in such emergencies. This point is borne out by the unilateral nature of recent American commitments to defend Latin-American countries against communist aggression. The threatened establishment of a Soviet-supported base of operations in Cuba prompted the United States for the first time to pledge itself openly to act in defense of other American governments.[5] On September 4, 1962, President Kennedy, although he refrained from any reference to the Monroe Doctrine, declared, "It continues to be the policy of the United States that the Castro regime will not be allowed to export its aggressive purposes by force. It will be prevented by whatever means may be necessary from taking action against any part of the Western Hemisphere." This warning was subsequently reiterated in similar terms. The intervention of the United States in the Dominican Republic in April, 1965, for the announced purpose of preventing a communist take-over reinforced this position. On May 2, 1965, President Johnson declared, "The American nations cannot, must not, and will not permit the establishment of

5. It should be noted that the United States has always maintained its complete liberty of action in supporting the Monroe Doctrine.

another communist government in the Western Hemisphere."

The chief *military* function of the OAS (as distinguished from the United States itself) is to serve as a vehicle for coordinating military policy under the leadership of the United States. The principal instrumentality of military assistance is the group of eighteen bilateral agreements between the United States and its allies. But even these agreements, although formally directed against communist aggression, are also intended to serve other political purposes such as precluding military assistance agreements with non-American countries and maintaining dominant access for the United States to the important military sector of Latin-American society.

In the development of American alliances, therefore, the OAS was significant for the hemispheric relations of the United States, but it was not primarily an instrumentality of American cold war policy, and it was not the model or precursor of subsequent American alliances.

3. *The Transformation of American Alliance Policy*

The great departure in American alliance policy was not the OAS but the North Atlantic Treaty of 1949. In becoming a party to this treaty the United States finally abandoned the no-permanent-alliance policy it had followed since the adoption of the Constitution, and it abandoned that policy in the very part of the world in which it had been regarded as peculiarly applicable.

The basic reason for American participation in the North Atlantic Treaty was simple enough. The treaty was concluded after it became apparent, during the Berlin blockade of 1948-49, that efforts toward economic reconstruction and political stability in Western Europe required a framework of security, if they were to prove effective, and that in the circumstances this security could only be provided by an

American pledge to defend Western Europe against a Soviet attack.

A European framework already existed and had received informal American support and participation. In the 1948 Treaty of Brussels the Western European allies of World War II had pledged themselves to a joint defense system and had decided to create a defense organization on the SHAEF pattern, with a permanent council, supreme commanders, and a collective force structure. All the determinants of an indigenous alliance seemed to be operating except one— sufficient military capability. Hence came the need for associating American military power with the Brussels Treaty states. Even so-called isolationists in the United States accepted the logic of association, but they wanted a less binding form of association than an alliance. Senator Taft, for example, suggested announcing a kind of Monroe Doctrine for Europe. But in light of the isolationist history of the United States and the conviction that a firm advance commitment to the defense of Europe was essential to avoid another world war with belated American intervention, the members of the Brussels pact and the Truman-Acheson administration believed that a formal alliance was essential to establish a credible American pledge of military assistance. Thus the North Atlantic Treaty was far more than an arrangement to provide the United States with air and naval bases. (The United States subsequently acquired bases in Spain, Libya, Morocco, and elsewhere without alliances.) At the same time, the alliance was a much less extensive commitment at the outset than it became after the Korean War.

In the beginning the North Atlantic Treaty was a guarantee pact that formally expressed, and thereby made unmistakably clear, America's vital interest in preserving the security and independence of the nations of Western Europe.[6]

6. On the face of it the treaty also embraced nonmilitary matters in pledging its signatories to settle disputes among themselves peacefully, to refrain from the threat or use of force in any way inconsistent with

The guarantee was embodied in Article V, in which the twelve parties (Belgium, Canada, Denmark, France, Iceland, Italy, Luxembourg, the Netherlands, Norway, Portugal, the United Kingdom, and the United States) agreed that "an armed attack against one or more of them in Europe or North America shall be considered an attack against them all" and promised assistance to the attacked member by "such action as [the assisting member] deems necessary, including the use of armed force." The original alliance contained no military or political organization, and none was anticipated. After the North Atlantic Treaty Organization was created, however, "NATO" came to designate the alliance as well as the organization (a designation that we shall generally follow for the sake of convenience).

In the context of Soviet-American rivalry, the treaty signified a clear acknowledgment by the United States that Soviet domination of Western Europe would shift the world balance of power decisively against the United States and thus open the Western Hemisphere to the encroachment of the adversary. At the very least, it was assumed that domination of Western Europe by the Soviet Union would create such a serious security problem for the United States as to severely strain the nation's resources and democratic institutions. Yet the military strategy for preventing Soviet aggression at first envisioned a much more limited role for the United States than it acquired after the Korean War. The strategy called for "an integrated defense of the North Atlantic area" in which the European allies would provide the ground forces and the United States would confine its contribution essentially to strategic bombing and protection of the sea lanes.

---

the principles of the United Nations, to develop friendly and peaceful international relations by strengthening free institutions, to eliminate conflict in their economic relations, and to encourage economic collaboration. In practice, however, these provisions were largely ignored. The alliance as such has played no part, for example, in trying to resolve the smoldering Greek-Turkish dispute over Cyprus.

If the basic motivation that led to this historic departure in American alliance policy seemed simple enough, the official rationale was less convincing in one respect. In responding to criticism of American participation in the North Atlantic Treaty, it went considerably beyond the basic security motive. Opposition to the treaty came from both "isolationists" and "internationalists." Whereas the one group recalled the past, the other group invoked a hoped-for future. To the former, NATO meant abandoning the nation's time-honored freedom of action in that it required, contrary to the Constitution of the United States and American tradition, a virtually automatic commitment to defend Western Europe against attack.[7] To the latter group, NATO meant abandoning the policy of achieving peace and security through the United Nations. Both criticisms converged in their insistence that NATO meant the acceptance of a policy of traditional military alliances, a policy based on the discredited principle of the balance of power.

The Truman administration was not insensitive to the criticism that NATO implied the abandonment of collective security and the acceptance of a balance of power policy. NATO was carefully distinguished from "traditional military alliances" and therefore from a balance of power policy,

---

7. In substance, this interpretation of the treaty was not far wrong. The deterrent value of the American commitment and the reassurance this commitment would give to the Western European states depended upon its certainty and its automaticity. This quality of automaticity was greatly reinforced later by the stationing of American ground forces in Europe and by the integration of the defenses of the parties to the North Atlantic Treaty, although the growth of Soviet strategic nuclear power called it into question. Technically, however, there was no automatic commitment, because the treaty left to each party the right to decide when an armed attack had taken place; even after a party had decided that an armed attack had taken place, it was not obliged to assist the attacked party with armed force.

and it was represented as an application of collective security.[8] The application was admittedly on a regional basis, but no contradiction was admitted between regional and universal collective security. Instead, the strengthening of regional security contributed, in this view, to the strengthening of universal security. Accordingly, NATO was described as an arrangement that was entirely consistent with the letter and spirit of the United Nations Charter—as, indeed, it was—and that contributed significantly toward strengthening the basic principles of the Charter.

4. *The High Point of the United Nations in American Expectations*

The persistence with which NATO was represented as an application of "collective security" presumably reflected a public opinion still averse to alliances and insistent on identifying foreign policy initiatives with supranational purposes and the procedures of the United Nations. This identification was facilitated in the early stages of the cold war by the composition of the membership in the United Nations and the dominance of the Western powers in the General Assembly. It was facilitated further by the fortuitous circumstances attending the outbreak of the Korean War, circumstances that permitted the Security Council to sanction the American action in Korea and thereby to give this action the character of a United Nations undertaking.

8. At the time of the Senate hearings on NATO, a State Department memorandum on the treaty rejected the contention that NATO was a "traditional military alliance." Instead, the memorandum declared that NATO was a pure application of collective security: "It is directed against no one; it is directed solely against aggression. It seeks not to influence any shifting 'balance of power' but to strengthen the 'balance of principle.' " Similar characterizations of the treaty were made by its principal advocates in the Senate.

These circumstances appeared so favorable at the time that they prompted the expectation that the United Nations might well serve the role of legitimizing American and Western policies and that "collective security" could indeed be made to coincide, if not in theory, then as a practical matter, with "collective defense." The high point of this expectation was marked late in 1950 when the General Assembly passed the Uniting for Peace resolution, sponsored by the United States, to enable the Assembly, without Security Council action, to sanction future collective measures in response to aggression.

As events were soon to demonstrate, this expectation proved too optimistic. Korea was the first and the last effort of collective defense against communist aggression to enjoy the sanction of the United Nations. With the increase in United Nations membership, an increase made up in large measure of states adhering to a policy of nonalignment, the expectations that Korea had nourished steadily declined, never to be revived. Instead, the prospect arose of a clash between the collective defense requirements of American policy and the General Assembly's interpretation of the requirements of the Charter. The United States did not abandon the United Nations after this transformation, but it did place less emphasis on finding in the United Nations a broader justification of American commitments, including alliances, and of the measures to which those commitments gave rise.

In the decade following the initiation of containment, the Korean War stands out as the decisive event in the evolution of American alliance policy. If the strategy of containment required the transformation of America's traditional alliance policy, it did not specify the nature of this transformation. More than any other event, the Korean experience determined the form American alliances eventually took. At the outbreak of the Korean War, it remained uncertain whether the United States would extend its commitments beyond the

Western Hemisphere and the North Atlantic region. Even within the area of commitment, the means by which America would implement its pledge to assist in the defense of Western Europe remained uncertain. Korea, for a long time to come, put an end to these uncertainties.

IV

ALLIANCES IN EUROPE

1. *The North Atlantic Treaty Organization*

The Korean War touched off a chain of events that consolidated the bipolar United States–U.S.S.R. deterrent balance in Europe and established American and Soviet forces along the iron curtain. The primary instrumentalities of these developments were two highly institutionalized multilateral alliances with important intra-alliance functions—alliances in which the superpowers held hegemonial yet increasingly qualified control. In its essentials this remains the determining structure of power, although military and political conditions have substantially changed within it.

The Korean War led to the first and last real effort of all the major allies in the North Atlantic alliance to build up their forces to levels specified by the military as being necessary to withstand a Soviet attack. It also led to the establishment of the treaty organization, with a council, an "integrated" military force, and a unified headquarters headed by an American commander—the permanent military organization envisaged by the Brussels Treaty powers. More than this, it soon led to the semipermanent stationing of American forces on the Continent, originally to encourage the European allies to meet their force goals and later to reinforce the credibility of America's guarantee. Finally, the repercussions of the Korean-born defense effort led in 1955 to West Germany's joining NATO.

With this enlargement and institutionalization of America's commitment to Europe, the United States became the dominant military power in Western Europe, intimately involved in the task of eliciting allied military contributions, fostering a strategic consensus, managing a common front during crises, orchestrating allied diplomatic positions and initiatives, and generally sustaining allied cohesion and security in response to changing military and political conditions. This role was a far cry from the original expectation that Western Europe would largely manage its own military affairs and from the abiding hope that it would federate and become an equal partner in an "Atlantic community."

Among peacetime alliances NATO is unprecedented in the extent of its co-ordination and centralization. Nevertheless, its vaunted "integration" falls far short of supranationalism. Essentially, integration in NATO means simply the co-ordination of forces and plans in peacetime so that they could more readily be employed under central command and control in wartime *if* the members agreed. But even the actual co-ordination of forces and logistics—except in air defense, where it is technically indispensable—is far from complete. The national military forces assigned to NATO are under sovereign national control until released by the national governments to the NATO command for authorized use. Only the Federal Republic of Germany does not formally possess a general staff of its own, but even its forces cannot be raised, deployed, or used without its assent. The use of an ally's territory and facilities by foreign forces is based on a network of bilateral agreements that prohibit their use against the will of the host country. The nuclear warheads assigned to NATO are under exclusive American control, although the weapons are under bilateral two-key arrangements. The great bulk of nuclear weapons upon which deterrence in Europe depends are outside Europe and under exclusive American control. Joint nuclear planning in NATO relates only to carrying out, not to determining, decisions made by the President of the United States.

More important than integration in determining NATO's essential characteristic is simply the fact that NATO is an institutionalized relationship in which the United States has held preponderant power and responsibility in the management of armed forces. Otherwise, integration could scarcely have existed. The multilateral institutions of the organization have facilitated co-ordination of American and allied forces and have made America's preponderance, including the holding of the principal military commands by Americans and the presence of American forces in Europe, more palatable. In the name of multilateral integration, the United States can see itself as the leading partner serving with the consent of a community of allies rather than as merely a dominant member of an old-fashioned coalition. The first conception is not only more congenial to American principles of international relations; it also enhances the claim of America's allies to have influence on American management. So the United States and most of its allies, eager to preserve the American presence in Europe, have come to think of the organization as the political as well as military condition of an effective American commitment. Yet, from the standpoint of making deterrence credible to the Soviet Union, the essential fact has certainly been American nuclear power and the presence of American forces in Europe to back the treaty's guarantee.

The concept of an integrated allied force sprang from the original strategy of a combined massive defense of Europe in a third world war. After the Korean War, that strategy was definitely abandoned, on unilateral American and British initiatives, in favor of a deterrent strategy that relied primarily on tactical and strategic nuclear responses to any aggression, even if it were non-nuclear. This new strategy persisted into the second half of the 1950's, even while the Soviet Union's capacity to devastate Europe and the United States grew impressively with the advent of thermonuclear warheads and long-range ballistic missiles. In the 1960's, especially during the Kennedy-McNamara administration, the United States again undertook a unilateral revision of NATO's strategy—this time in the direction of "controlled and flexible response," which included raising the threshold of resort to nuclear weapons in Europe. This strategy, however, received little more than reluctant conceptual endorsement by America's allies and outright opposition by France. Only West Germany yielded to America's prodding of its allies to build up their contribution to a "forward defense" and created twelve army divisions. The net result of America's strategic revision was to gain more explicit recognition in the alliance of the function of low-level, short-term, non-nuclear resistance to deter a conventional *fait accompli* and to withstand a very limited conventional encounter that might grow out of miscalculations in a crisis. In effect, NATO's military security remained as dependent as before on nuclear deterrence, supplemented physically by a somewhat larger conventional trip-wire and reinforced psychologically by the prospect that any military encounter in Europe would quickly escalate to the nuclear level. Consequently, France's withdrawal of its forces from NATO assignment and command in 1966 did not have a serious *military* impact upon either the organization or the alliance, and it tended only to reinforce existing military trends.[1]

Logically one might suppose, as some analysts have alleged, that NATO's continuing dependence on the American nuclear force, although the Soviet Union not only has the capacity to devastate Europe but is increasing its ability to attack the United States as well, would so undermine the confidence of allies in the willingness of the United States to

1. The military consequences of France's withdrawal are examined in detail in Brigadier K. Hunt, "NATO Without France: The Military Implications" (Adelphi Papers, no. 32, Institute for Strategic Studies, December 1966).

risk its cities for the sake of theirs that the original basis for the alliance would be nullified and threatened with obsolescence. Indeed, the growth of Soviet nuclear power, in conjunction with United States emphasis on a "controlled and flexible response," did raise serious doubts, especially in Germany and France, about the reliability of the American guarantee. But to conclude that these doubts render the alliance obsolete is to carry the peculiar logic of hypothetical nuclear exchanges too far. Not only does this logic underestimate the appeal of the intra-alliance functions of NATO; it also overestimates the clarity and intensity of the calculations that governments and nations make about military security in the nuclear age. The fact of the matter is that the European allies have maintained sufficient confidence in the efficacy of nuclear deterrence to regard the American guarantee as operational. Some reasons for this confidence are: the allies' conviction that no state will deliberately take the slightest risk of war when war could mean nuclear devastation, their low estimate of Soviet military intentions in Europe, the demonstrated will of the United States to resist Soviet incursions in Berlin and Cuba, and the impressive magnitude and scope of America's nuclear power. Moreover, the alternatives to depending primarily on America's nuclear deterrent have not proved to be as attractive as the distinctly French arguments for an independent nuclear force asserted that they would be. Even the French government apparently does not regard its nuclear force as a substitute for America's force, however dispensable it may regard its alliance with the United States.

If NATO is going to erode into impotence, the very confidence of the allies in the efficacy of nuclear deterrence—confidence that could become complacency—seems more likely to speed the process than a lack of confidence in America's nuclear guarantee. For, in time, the allies may become convinced that the North Atlantic Treaty by itself is almost automatically a sufficient guarantee of security and that no continuing give-and-take on military and political matters of common concern—and certainly no institutional superstructure or integrated military forces—are necessary to maintain the guarantee's vitality. The continuation of détente into the 1970's would tend to reinforce this outlook.

2. NATO in Détente

In the period of détente that set in sporadically after Khrushchev's accession to power and more steadily in the aftermath of the Cuban missile crisis, military security and military strategy ceased to be the primary concern of the allies. Détente evidently did not constitute a Soviet-American *rapprochement* or even a political truce. It did not settle any substantive issues in contest between the two states. Détente did not preclude oscillations in Soviet-American tensions. Indeed, it included the possibility of a revival of Soviet political and diplomatic offensives aimed at exploiting divisions among the Western allies.

Outside Europe détente showed no promise of diminishing the more or less continual effort of the Soviet Union since 1955 to establish a dominant political position among the Arab countries, and even the northern tier countries, of the Middle East. Détente did, however, represent the mutual interest of the superpowers in avoiding confrontations that might lead to their direct involvement in war with each other, and it represented the Soviet Union's interest in avoiding commitments to revolutionary movements that might only redound to Chinese advantage or impose claims on Soviet assistance with little prospect of enhancing Soviet power.

In Europe, détente reflected Soviet acceptance, however reluctant and tentative, of a situation of economic, political, and military strength among the Western states that made incursions like the Berlin crises seem unprofitable. At the same time, American strength and political will to resist sudden changes in the military status quo elsewhere, as demonstrated in the Cuban missile crisis, made attempts to gain leverage against Western Europe from outside Europe seem dangerously counterproductive. Under the circumstances, Soviet leaders saw détente as the best way to consolidate the status quo in the center of Europe, diminish American influence, and encourage the disbandment of NATO.

One effect of détente was to reduce greatly the expectation of an imminent Soviet political or military offensive in Europe that would require the use—direct or indirect—of countervailing military power. This change of expectation raised, in turn, the fundamental questions of whether the structures of power and order that were created in Europe in response to the most intense phase of the cold war could survive a reduction of that vital stimulus and, if not, what new pattern of international relations would ensue while these old structures crumbled. In Western Europe, in particular, the presumably reduced military urgency, if not utility, of NATO raised the questions of whether this institutionalized alliance would continue to command the cooperation necessary to preserve its basic cohesion as a deterrent to Soviet probes and crises and whether it would continue to perform intra-alliance political functions that had come to the forefront with the economic and political revival of Europe. In a period of minimal concern about military security, the internal political problems of the alliance seemed to pose a conspicuous challenge to its vitality.

From the beginning, one of the organization's primary political functions, especially important for United States policy, was to tie West Germany into the Western community, enlarged by American membership, in such a way that it could regain something of its inherent power and status while remaining under constraints so as not to frighten its neighbors. This was also Germany's policy. Hence, Germany and the United States were the most ardent champions of integration.

Germany's integration in NATO was particularly crucial

because of its rearmament, which began in 1956. After the demise of the European Defense Community (EDC), which would have integrated German forces into a European army below the division level, all of Germany's military forces were "placed under the authority" of NATO's military headquarters (SHAPE) and "assigned" to NATO command. Thus NATO assumed the function of constraining Germany, for which EDC had been designed.

In joining NATO, Germany accepted certain special constraints in return for greater security against the Soviet bloc, the allies' recognition of its full statehood, and their pledge to achieve "through peaceful means . . . a fully free and unified Germany." The explicit constraints were (1) Germany's unilateral abnegation of the production on its soil of atomic and other weapons of mass destruction, (2) its authorization for stationing allied forces on its territory, and (3) its acceptance of continued rights and responsibilities of the United States, Britain, and France "relating to Berlin and to Germany as a whole, including the reunification of Germany and a peace settlement." But equally significant were all the implicit constraints springing from Germany's effort to overcome its vulnerable geographical position, the stigma of its history, and above all its division. These constraints, it sometimes seemed to Germans, were aimed at guaranteeing Germany's good behavior. In any case, they made Germany unusually dependent upon its allies' good favor.

Thus, with respect to Germany, NATO served a special function of intra-alliance control. In a broader sense, NATO, throughout the alliance, has served functions of control that are tantamount to functions of international order. NATO became a framework for concerting, or at least bargaining over and compromising, military policies—a realm of vital interests traditionally pursued in Western Europe by unfettered national autonomy and competing alliances. The dominant role of the United States in

NATO's military posture thus removed what was historically a major source of conflict and war. Consequently, the European members of NATO, conscious of the contrast between their postwar harmony and prewar discord, tended to view their interdependence in NATO as a safeguard against reversion to a more dangerous, fragmented pattern of relations.

National differences among allies continued to exist, of course, but they were not expressed in competitive arming. They were reflected in differing military policies, although these policies were directed toward countering the Soviet Union, not other Western European states. The process of trying to sustain a satisfactory balance of liabilities and benefits for a number of allied states over a long period during which the threat of aggression did not seem imminent tended to focus attention upon these differences among allies. A striking example of this internalization of allied concern was the sensitive and agitated issue of nuclear control, which related far more directly to the confidence, power, and status of allies—particularly Germany—than to their security against an external threat.

Naturally, in matters of interallied politics the United States played the major role and was the major focus of allied pressure for more advantageous terms of collaboration. Naturally, too, the members of NATO found their dependence upon the United States irksome in various degrees, whatever the advantages might be. Basically, this was due to the economic and political resurgence of old, proud, and cohesive states eager to express their national individuality. Some allies doubted the wisdom, in the long run, of depending exclusively on America's nuclear deterrent when the Soviet capacity to devastate the United States seemed bound to increase and when the United States was involved in demanding tasks of containment outside Europe. But it was more important, in the circumstances of détente, that their very *confidence* in the stability of the balance of terror and

in the apparent diminution of the Soviet military threat increased their dissatisfaction with their dependence on the
United States and encouraged them to express it. In the late
1960's, therefore, security considerations became quite subordinate in the eyes of European allies to their growing dissatisfaction (in Germany and Italy, as well as France) with
the disparity of power—technological-industrial as well as
military and diplomatic—between them and the United
States and their anxiety that American preponderance and
wealth might consign them permanently to a second-rate status. Their dissatisfaction and anxiety were aggravated by the
fear that United States–Soviet co-operation, as in the proposed nuclear nonproliferation treaty, might operate in such
a way as to discriminate against the allies in a whole range of
military, political, and technological matters.

The chief response of the United States to this shift of the
allies' concern was to offer them a greater share of information about, and perhaps influence upon, military planning
and strategy. But in the nature of things there were severe
limits on the extent to which any state—and especially one
with such preponderant power and responsibility as the
United States—could be expected to share control of its
decision-making processes. It is doubtful that the most far-
reaching effort to share nuclear power, the proposed multilateral force (MLF)—which encountered insuperable political opposition from France, Britain, and Russia, largely
because of Germany's prospective membership—would
actually have given its members more than a claim for somewhat greater influence upon American decisions. Moreover,
no amount of sharing or consultation could alleviate the
root cause of allied dissatisfaction—the great military-
technological superiority of the United States, a foreign
power acting as the leader of their alliance on their own
continent.

Consequently, barring a revival of Soviet offensive pressure, there was little prospect that the centrifugal forces in

the alliance would elicit compensatory measures of co-ordination and integration. Instead, the significant tendency was toward increased political independence and mobility on the part of the major allies within an atmosphere of minimal, and in some cases negligible, concern with military security. France's withdrawal from the organization and the willingness of the allies—even eagerness, on Germany's part—to maintain as much co-operation with her as possible while minimizing the significance of her defection, rendered the elaborate superstructure of the alliance more conspicuously an American instrumentality that was losing its military value except, perhaps, for maintaining United States-German collaboration.

Inevitably, the erosion of the organization's military functions also called its political utility into question. Even without the organization, the United States, with Germany's co-operation, might readily safeguard Western Europe's military security. But would the alliance continue to perform its internal political functions if the organization eroded? Would the dismantling of NATO's superstructure and the apparent reduction of the military need for it enable the allies to order their relations with more self-reliance, or would it only give freer rein to the tensions among them?

The answer to this question would depend significantly upon the reaction of the United States to the loosening of NATO's bonds. Would the United States continue to carry the burdens of preponderance for the sake of containing Germany and performing other intra-alliance functions if the military rationale of the formal structure of military co-operation seemed unconvincing? Was America's withdrawal —officially called redeployment—of some of its forces from Europe in 1967 merely a limited adjustment to technological realities (particularly greater capabilities of direct airlift from the United States) and economic pressures (especially the balance-of-payments problem), or did it foreshadow a further reduction of American forces to a purely symbolic presence and, perhaps, the dismantling of the whole superstructure of the alliance through its repercussions on other allies? If the United States were to withdraw all but a symbolic military presence from Europe, with or without comparable Soviet withdrawals, might the relations of the European states revert to historical patterns of competitive arming and separate alliances? Probably not. Nevertheless, the conditions of security and order in Western Europe would almost certainly change radically.

Even without the erosion of NATO or the withdrawal of America's military presence, the consolidation of détente and the revival of political and diplomatic mobility in Europe were bound to focus allied attention on the outstanding political problem in the alliance—how to contain West Germany, closely tied to a Western alliance, while satisfying its basic national objectives, particularly the unification of Germany. Under the Kennedy administration the United States began advising Germany to be less "rigid" in its policy toward East Europe. In 1966 the West German government, with American and allied approval, abandoned the old formula for reunification, which envisaged a grand negotiated settlement from a position of strength based upon West Germany's tight integration into a Western community, and adopted the American formula of "peaceful engagement," which looked toward reunification as the end result of a slow process of building closer relations between East and West Europe. In accordance with the new atmosphere of diplomatic flexibility accompanying this political departure, a new German administration launched a more active and independent policy, which looked not only toward a revival of the abortive Franco-German *rapprochement* of 1963,[2] but also toward closer relations with states to the East.

2. In January, 1963, President de Gaulle and Chancellor Adenauer signed the Franco-German Treaty of Friendship. Adenauer's retire-

Considering the limits to what Germany could accomplish in either direction, it remained to be seen whether its new diplomacy marked a healthy change from immobilism and overdependence on the United States or whether it might eventually lead to frustration and some kind of extreme domestic or foreign policy reaction in a vain effort to break away from unyielding political constraints. If German expectations were to be confined to improving the conditions of political life in East Germany and slowly creating a new constellation of East-West interests and alignments within which closer official relations between the two Germanies could come about without formally freezing the territorial status quo, NATO would probably retain its vitality as an essential framework for reconciling détente with the accommodation of German nationalism. But if the Federal Republic's Eastern initiatives led only to recognition of the GDR or otherwise frustrated rising expectations, its national disappointment might be directed against NATO and toward some radical solution. If this disaffection were accompanied by a burst of East German nationalism, the problem of integrating the two Germanies into a stable international environment would become so acute as to threaten the security and order of Europe itself.

The effects of détente and the loosening of NATO's ties upon Germany's position therefore raised larger questions: Would the alliance, transformed from a guarantee pact to a semi-integrated military organization at a time of apparent military urgency, continue to function during a protracted détente as a framework of interallied order and external security? Could it function on the basis of American military preponderance? If not, would some more suitable framework for order and security emerge? Would the essentially bipolar

---

ment and the succession of Ludwig Erhard, followed by France's strong opposition to Erhard's pro-American stance in supporting the MLF project, largely destroyed the atmosphere of co-operation represented in the treaty.

military balance of power in Europe be replaced by a multipolar balance, or would it merely be qualified by greater diplomatic movement within and across alliances? Might détente eventually lead to some kind of settlement of the division of Germany, followed by a political-military realignment on an entirely new basis?

The answers to these questions depend not only upon developments within the North Atlantic alliance, but also upon the interaction of these developments with developments outside the alliance, especially in the Soviet bloc.

3. The Warsaw Treaty Organization

On the other side of the somewhat eroded iron curtain, the Soviet Union is not only the manager of military power; it has dominated the internal as well as external affairs of the states in its Eastern European bloc. Whereas the North Atlantic alliance began as a purely externally directed guarantee pact and became a framework of interallied relations as well as a semi-integrated coalition for security, the Soviet Union's postwar bilateral defense treaties with the East European satellites began as a network of links in a virtual empire. After the establishment of the Warsaw Treaty Organization (WTO) in 1955, however, these treaties acquired some of the features of a multilateral military coalition under qualified Soviet hegemony.

In the ten years before the WTO was established, Stalin created a network of formal political, military, economic, and cultural arrangements with what could then be called Soviet "satellites," including no less than 329 bilateral treaties, agreements, and protocols. Moscow pledged military assistance in bilateral pacts with all the East European states except Albania and East Germany (GDR). These pacts generally provided for *casus foederis* in the event of aggression against either signatory by a resurgent Germany or by states supporting Germany. To these were added bilateral pacts among the East European states themselves (although Moscow denounced the pact with Yugoslavia in September, 1949, and all the satellites except Albania followed suit) and a series of friendship and co-operation treaties.

Under Russian influence the military forces of Eastern Europe were gradually molded into separate yet subordinate arms of the Soviet military establishment. Noncommunist and Titoist officers were purged and replaced by officers drawn from the ranks of the Party or indoctrinated after the war. Sovietization reached its peak during the Korean War when East European forces reached a total of 1,500,000 men. Yet before the Warsaw Pact there seems to have been little integration or even joint maneuvers between these and Soviet forces.

While Soviet military arrangements rested exclusively on bilateral pacts prior to 1955, multilateral bases for political and economic co-operation were established in the Communist Information Bureau (Cominform) and the Council of Mutual Economic Assistance (CEMA), which was Moscow's answer to the Marshall Plan.[3] Actually, however, neither of these organizations added anything significant to Soviet unilateral and bilateral influence.

Multilateralism in Soviet military relations with East Europe began with the establishment of the WTO in May, 1955; the Warsaw Pact was signed by Moscow and all the East European members of the socialist camp including the GDR, but excluding Yugoslavia. The *casus foederis* of the WTO is an "armed attack in Europe" upon any one

3. The Cominform's main function turned out to be the mobilization of opposition against Tito's Yugoslav Party until the Soviet-Yugoslav reconciliation in 1956. CEMA's ostensible purpose was to co-ordinate economic, joint investment, and production plans and to facilitate the division of productive labor. However, under Stalin's policy of national autarchy and the exploitation of satellite economics through bilateral pacts, it was basically inactive except for promoting intrabloc trade. In 1954-56, CEMA began to work toward the co-ordination of its members' five-year plans.

or more signatories of the treaty by "any state or group of states." The contracting parties are obliged to come to the assistance of any victim with all means deemed necessary by them, including armed force. They agree to consult with one another "on all important issues affecting their common interests" and in case of "a threat of armed attack on one or more of the Parties . . . ." Article VII obliges the signatories to forsake all other "coalitions, or alliances . . . [or] agreements whose objects conflict with the object of the treaty." The signatories also pledge themselves to work for the peaceful settlement of disputes, for disarmament, and for the conclusion of an all-European security treaty. Articles V and VI provide for two mechanisms to implement the treaty—a joint military command and a political consultative committee.

A joint command was created in a separate protocol and could therefore legally remain in force even if the WTO were to be merged in a general European treaty. The protocol provided that "general questions relating to the strengthening of the defensive power and the organization of the Joint Armed Forces of the signatory states" should be decided by the political consultative committee. Soviet Marshal Konev was made "Commander-in-chief of the Joint Armed Forces to be assigned by the signatory states," while military leaders from the member states would serve as his deputies and command the forces that were assigned to the joint armed forces from their own countries. A staff of the joint armed forces was to be set up in Moscow. And—a key provision—"the disposition of the Joint Armed Forces in the territories of the signatory states" was to be effected "by agreement among the states, in accordance with the requirements of their mutual defense." The participation of East Germany, which did not yet have a defense ministry or formal sovereignty, was to be "examined at a later date." A meeting of the political consultative committee in January, 1956, announced that "organizational problems concerning activities of the unified armed forces" from WTO members "were solved." A decision was also taken to include the GDR army in the "unified armed forces." Soviet forces, however, were stationed only in the GDR, Hungary, Poland, and Rumania, and not in Albania, Bulgaria, or Czechoslovakia. They were withdrawn from Rumania in 1958.

In reality, the WTO, although established in the form of a military alliance against an armed attack, served intra-alliance functions primarily and military security only indirectly. Except for some modernization of East European forces from 1955 to 1960, Moscow was slow to develop the military potential of non-Soviet forces. Not until 1961 were there firm reports of joint WTO maneuvers. The WTO was in part a propaganda and bargaining device, created to retaliate against West Germany for joining NATO and to execute a threat intended (in conjunction with the model of the Austrian State Treaty) to discourage that event. Basically, it became a device to impose, justify, and retain Soviet controls and Soviet forces and cadre in Eastern Europe. Significantly, the Kremlin justified the use of Soviet forces to suppress the Hungarian uprising in 1956 in terms of the Warsaw Treaty, pointing to its members' pledge under Article V "to take the agreed measures necessary to strengthen their defense, to protect the peaceful labor of their peoples, guarantee the integrity of their borders and territories, and guarantee defense from possible aggression."

Yet the Hungarian debacle and signs of disaffection in other WTO nations led Moscow to try to preserve the essential cohesion of its bloc by more subtle controls and by cautious concessions to national individuality. One of its first moves in this direction was to sign status-of-forces agreements with Warsaw, Budapest, Bucharest, and Pankow.[4]

4. The agreement with Poland declared that the presence of Soviet troops should in no way impair the sovereignty of the Polish state and that Soviet troops were not to interfere in Poland's internal affairs. It further provided for special agreements to specify the number of So-

In 1961 Moscow showed increasing interest in transforming its East European alliance into a more effective and coordinated military structure by introducing modern weapons (including tactical rockets capable of using nuclear warheads), joint maneuvers, and further integration of doctrine, training, equipment, and planning. Although the WTO governments welcomed modernization of their armies, they apparently placed limits on tighter organization under Soviet command. There were also signs that these governments were pressing for a more influential voice in matters affecting their own interests, such as military strategy, the sharing of military and economic burdens, and major foreign policy issues.[5] So along with the modernization and integration of the WTO there was pressure from its members for an assured contractual and bargaining relationship with the Soviet Union.

As a military organization the WTO was significant chiefly among the northern tier countries—Poland, the GDR, and Czechoslovakia—where there were useful military forces and a consensus about the circumstances in which they might be used, especially in the event of West German aggression. Yet the actual efficacy of the WTO as an instrument of political control, which depends largely on the political influence and reliability of the East European military establishments, must remain in some doubt in the absence of a test case.

---

viet troops on Polish soil and their location; to regulate legal aid regarding crimes and misdemeanors by Soviet personnel; to determine the communication lines, time limits, procedures, and terms of payment for transit of Soviet troops and military property through Polish territory. In essence, troop movements, training, and maneuvers outside the base area were made contingent upon Polish agreement. A mixed Polish-Soviet Commission was set up to settle disputes arising from the treaty.

5. Thomas W. Wolfe, *The Evolving Nature of the Warsaw Pact* (Santa Monica, California: RAND Corporation, 1965), Report RM-4835-PR.

In the 1960's the Warsaw Treaty, like NATO, showed increasing evidence of allied restiveness and pressure in an atmosphere of relative military security. The most serious political tensions resulting from this revival of national self-assertion were, initially, those occasioned by the allies' search for status and independence with respect to their super-power, the Soviet Union.

Rumania, playing the role of France in NATO, took the lead in attacking the WTO as an instrument of Soviet preponderance and in championing the independence of allies. Beginning in 1958, after the withdrawal of Russian troops, it asserted its independence in a cautious step-by-step manner intended to test the limits of safe and successful maneuver. By April, 1966, Rumanian Party Secretary Nicolae Ceausescu was sufficiently bold to join with Tito in asserting that "the division of the world into military blocs does not correspond to the positive development of current international relations." Although Bucharest did not seek the termination of the Warsaw Pact, Rumanian leaders did propose far-reaching reforms in a Gaullist direction.[6] Furthermore, in January, 1967, Bucharest established diplomatic relations with West Germany against the Kremlin's wishes and over the protests of East German Chairman Walter Ulbricht.

Rumania's independent course is chiefly a product of growing economic strength and a stable, unified political regime basing its appeal on resurgent nationalism. It has been facilitated by the diminution of East-West tension and,

6. First, they wanted the command of the alliance rotated among all member states instead of going automatically to a Soviet marshal. Second, they insisted on the need for unanimity in pact decisions and demanded that the use of nuclear arms from the territory of a member state be subject to its consent. Third, they called for revision of the principles of financial contributions for the support of Soviet forces in East Germany, Poland, and Hungary so that their cost would be borne only by the countries involved instead of by all pact members.

to a lesser degree, by the leverage provided by the Sino-Soviet split. In varying degrees these same factors are working for the increased independence of other East European regimes.

However, the reassertion of national independence in the Soviet bloc is limited by divergencies within the bloc. Thus Rumania's recognition of West Germany led the GDR to form countervailing bilateral pacts of diplomatic consultation and co-operation with other bloc states. To a degree the Soviet Union has exploited such intra-alliance differences as a means of checking defection from its own policies. More important, national centrifugal tendencies in the bloc are substantially qualified by recognition of continuing Soviet hegemony in matters of ultimate security. There is no movement toward new military alignments nor even toward the withdrawal of the Soviet military presence in East Europe. Like the resurgence of national individuality in the policies of the West European allies, greater scope for independent maneuver in East Europe seems to depend on retention of a secure association with the power base provided by the superpower.

In response to this reassertion of nationalism, the question of Soviet determination to remain preponderant in Eastern Europe, in contrast to doubts about the permanence of America's presence in Western Europe, scarcely arises. The Soviet Union, unlike the United States, conceives of itself as necessarily a political and military power in Europe—dominant in the East and a primary influence in the West. It is primarily the latent Soviet threat to Western Europe that keeps the United States there, but the Soviet Union would be in Eastern Europe anyway, to check Germany, to await opportunities for political penetration westward, and to maintain an orderly group of buffer states in the Soviet commonwealth.

Yet, being determined to remain a European power, the Soviet Union has gone far to accommodate the changing political conditions of this status. It has acquiesced to a degree of allied divergence that would have been completely unacceptable before the Hungarian uprising. It even seems willing to grant a regularized relationship with its allies in which clearly sovereign, though vastly weaker, states are able to bargain with the superpower on a government-to-government basis. On the other hand, the persistence of East European fears of a resurgent West Germany and the continued unwillingness of Moscow to share control of tactical nuclear weapons or to extend allied participation in the collective instrumentalities of the WTO in other ways narrowly limit the extent to which the Soviet Union will respond to centrifugal developments by genuine "sharing."

As in NATO, the loosening of allied cohesion in the Soviet bloc during a period of relative military security raises the question of what impact this development might eventually have on the relations of the allies with each other. As in NATO, although by different means, the preponderance of the superpower has helped to suppress divergencies among allies that were intense and often violent in other periods of history. By comparison with the NATO countries, however, the ties of culture and politics checking these divergencies in East Europe are fragile. Historically a battleground between Russian and German drives for ascendancy, these states were no more inclined to build regional unity when they were relatively secure from Russian or German hegemony than when (as in the 1930's) they were menaced by a common enemy. Consequently, the loosening of Soviet controls and the reassertion of national individualities in East Europe, together with new opportunities for independent diplomatic and economic relations with West Germany, France, and other Western states, raise the uncertain specter of a new Balkanization of the area. This could lead to disorder and violence that would be hard to contain and possibly even to a disturbing Soviet attempt to restore order forcibly. For this reason Western states are generally anxious not to stimulate the nationalist forces in East Europe beyond the limits of an orderly progression toward greater internal and external freedom for WTO members within the existing structure of power. Yet in 1967 the specter of national anarchy seems almost as remote and hypothetical in East as in West Europe. Indeed, that specter tends to perpetuate the essential cohesion of the WTO as an institutionalized framework for the changing relationships among its members.

4. *The Persistence of a Bipolar Order*

In 1967, NATO and WTO remain opposing multilateral frameworks of political-military alignment within which the United States and the Soviet Union, respectively, are the preponderant (and, in the Soviet case, exclusive) managers of the military balance. The growing restiveness of some of the allies in both alliances toward their dependence on the superpowers in a period of détente might modify or erode the institutions of the alliances; but the very lack of concern with military security that détente reflects removes a major incentive to organize alternative military combinations, while the divisions among the allies, now accentuated by the same resurgence of national individuality that challenged the superpowers' hegemonies, are additional obstacles to such combinations.

The continuing bipolar military balance in Europe appears to be very stable as a deterrent to actions that either side might take at even a slight conscious risk of war. From the West's standpoint, deterrence is based on the unwillingness of the Soviet Union to run the literally incalculable risk that any aggression might lead to a nuclear war and on the certainty that a strategic nuclear war would result in devastation of the Soviet homeland (unless it were fought on an extremely restricted no-cities bargaining basis, which Soviet strategists regard as impossible). There are no signs that the growing capacity of the Soviet Union to devastate the

United States on a second strike encourages it to be more adventurous in approaching the brink of war. Moreover, Moscow's revival of tensions in Europe would interfere with its present political strategy, based on détente.

From the East's standpoint, the deterrence of Western (chiefly German) incursions depends on the Soviet Union rather than on the WTO as such. There are no signs that any of the Soviet Union's allies aspire to participate in the management of the military balance or that the Soviet Union would be willing to share any aspect of management. Rumania's defection, in contrast to France's, does not even extend to a desire to seek political leverage through independent military influence.

Thus the United States and the U.S.S.R. maintain the military framework of security and détente within which their allies, partly by virtue of the very stability of the military balance, can safely pursue somewhat divergent policies without having to assume the burdens of military management—and also without running much risk that the superpowers will withdraw their protection, since neither would be willing to concede such a victory to the other or to incur the consequent risks of disorder in its sphere of influence. One might describe this situation as political polycentrism within a framework of military duopoly.

The fact that the military balance in Europe is essentially a two-state balance simplifies the maintenance of mutual deterrence. Consequently, although bipolarity leaves the superpowers with the troublesome task of preserving the cohesion and security of their alliances when the incentives for independence are rising, they instinctively resist the emergence of new centers of military power and decisions. Although each tries to incite and exploit centrifugal tendencies within its adversary's alliance, neither wishes to see the European balance complicated by the appearance of new parties to the game. Both are anxious to avoid having their hands forced by catalytic or triggering actions of their allies.

To this extent each has an interest in its opponent's restraint of allies—a situation that does not escape the notice of the allies, who are inclined to suspect that collusion between the superpowers will be at their expense. However, the collusion does not extend much further than maintaining a military duopoly. Soviet leaders evidently regard the loosening of NATO and the new fluidity in European political life not as an opportunity to form a general peace-keeping concert with the United States, or even to bring about a mutually satisfactory European settlement with the West, but rather as an opportunity to supplant American influence in Europe with Soviet primacy. Consequently, the limited détente of the 1960's does not foreshadow the kind of basic realignment of principal contestants that would make obsolete the structures of power that developed in a more intense period of the cold war. It only emphasizes the intra-alliance function of these structures—namely, providing secure frameworks for changing political relationships among allied governments and people.

In 1967 it is difficult to see what would change this basic situation of polycentrism within bipolarity. Yet its perpetuation would be a great historical anomaly. It would mean that the whole area of East and West Europe—historically a region in which the major states have supported independent diplomatic maneuvers with military power organized in shifting patterns of alliances—would be content indefinitely with a kind of nonmilitary politics guaranteed by two semipermanent alliances under the dominant military management of extraregional states. It would mean that the traditional modes of international politics among these advanced states had been transformed because one vital element, the pursuit of military security, had been entrusted to two superpowers. Therefore, one must wonder: Can this state of affairs be anything more than a transitional stage between an eroding bipolarity and some new, more pluralistic and loosely organized pattern of alliances? Or might European nations simply cease to be concerned primarily with the stakes of politics for which their independent military power seems too ineffectual or too dangerous? Might interstate politics even become less important than transnational, functional politics in the life of European peoples?

Whatever the future pattern of European politics might be, it seems unlikely to replicate previous patterns. Correspondingly, the role of alliances will be different.

CHAPTER
V

ALLIANCES
OUTSIDE EUROPE

1. *The Extension of Containment to the Eurasian Periphery*

Before the Korean War the only areas thought to warrant direct American military support were the NATO area, Latin America, and the defense perimeter running from Japan, through the Philippines, to Australia. The Communists' victory on the Chinese mainland violated America's traditional interest in promoting an independent, united, but democratic (and therefore presumably friendly) China, and it touched off a virulent domestic controversy. But the United States had never contemplated supporting this interest with force before World War II and did not now consider abandoning the familiar postulate that American forces should refrain from becoming involved in a land war in Asia.

The magnitude of the task of shoring up the Kuomintang on the mainland seemed to make analogies to containment in Greece inapplicable. Furthermore, American military plans were based on the premise that in another general war—the only kind of war that plans envisaged—the Asian mainland would be a secondary theater, as in World War II. The maintenance of American forces in Korea, which the United States occupied for a few years as one of the legacies of the war, was regarded as an unnecessary diversion of limited forces from the Western Hemisphere and Europe. The United States resisted suggestions from the governments of the United Kingdom, Australia, the Philippines, and the Chinese Nationalists that it take the initiative in forming mutual defense arrangements against China in Southeast Asia.

Before the United States intervened in Korea, the cold war was almost wholly a European conflict, in American eyes. Yet, as that intervention revealed, the logic of the Truman Doctrine and the policy of containment could be applied to communist aggression in any other part of the world just as well. In retrospect it is not surprising, therefore, that the Korean War set off a chain of events that drastically altered American alliance policy not only in Europe, but also in the Asian-Pacific area and, to a lesser extent, in the Middle East. It led the United States to apply containment against China for the first time and to extend the geographical scope of containment against the Soviet Union. As in Europe, a primary instrumentality of containment was the formation of alliances. Basically, America's extension of alliances to the Eurasian periphery sprang from its effort to project and reinforce the credible deterrent power of the United States nuclear force, although the new alliances were supplemented by military assistance agreements to build local positions of military strength with local forces.

The Korean War showed that the United States, contrary to its previous strategy, might see a vital interest in opposing local aggression, even in an outlying position in Asia, because of its interest in the larger problem of containing the expansion of the communist domain. The North Korean invasion, following the omission of Korea from the officially stated defense perimeter in the Pacific, was attributed to a failure to make this interest clear in advance. As Secretary of State Dulles put it, "Peace requires anticipating what it is that tempts an aggressor and letting him know in advance that, if he does not exercise self-control, he may face a hard fight, perhaps a losing fight. The Korean War—the third such war in our generation—should finally have taught us that, if we can foresee aggression which causes us to fight, we should let this be known, so that the potential aggressor will take this into calculation."[1]

2. Asia

This principle of deterrence was first applied through alliances with South Korea, with the Chinese on Formosa, and with Japan, the Philippines, Australia, and New Zealand after the Korean War. In 1954, by a logical extension, it was applied to Southeast Asia after the French defeat in Indochina. The instrumentality of deterrence in the latter case was the Southeast Asia Collective Defense Treaty (commonly referred to as SEATO), signed by the United States, Australia, New Zealand, the United Kingdom, France, the Philippines, Thailand, and Pakistan. The treaty applied to the "general area of South Asia," including three nonsignatories: South Vietnam, Laos, and Cambodia.[2]

The Eisenhower-Dulles administration hoped that, given the clarification of American interests by means of these alliances, coupled with the more explicit intention to apply a strategy of massive and selective nuclear retaliation against direct Chinese aggression or Soviet-supported attacks on the Eurasian periphery, American nuclear power would be a sufficient deterrent and would spare the United States the problem of preparing to fight a series of local wars at points of communist choosing. It recognized that this kind of deterrence would leave open the possibility of indirect aggression by unconventional war and subversion. Yet, although the SEATO treaty made allowances for mutual assistance against subversion, no one then expected that such subversion would eventually involve American forces.

1. *Department of State Bulletin*, no. 742, September 14, 1953.
2. These three states, although not parties to the treaty, were placed under the terms of the treaty by a protocol. Cambodia soon rejected SEATO protection. Laos was neutralized by the Geneva agreement of 1962.

In the aftermath of the Korean War, American participation in a land war in Asia was even more "unthinkable" than before. Accordingly, the United States had declined to put its ground forces into Indochina, although, in official statements comparing the loss of Indochina to a row of falling dominoes, it had acknowledged a vital interest in preventing a communist victory in that area. The United States had rejected requests from Australia, New Zealand, and the Philippines to station mobile forces at key points on the Asian periphery. The post-Korean alliances in Asia were even more purely an instrument of nuclear deterrence than NATO, for in Europe, at least, the United States acknowledged the need of a conventional capability with an American component. Yet, beyond their deterrent function, these alliances bore little resemblance to NATO.

The first set of alliances, formed in 1951, reinforced the old defense perimeter. The Mutual Defense Treaty with the Philippines and the Tripartite Treaty with Australia and New Zealand, known as the ANZUS pact, define the *casus foederis* as an "armed attack in the Pacific Area" (including island territories, armed forces, and public vessels and aircraft of the signatories). But the obligation to respond to attack is defined much less rigorously than in the North Atlantic Treaty. The signatories simply recognize that an attack on any of them would be dangerous to all and declare that each would "meet the common danger in accordance with its constitutional processes." Although principally directed against Russia and China, the ANZUS pact also reflected Australia's and New Zealand's desire to marshal American power as assurance against the revival of Japanese expansion.

The treaties of peace and security with Japan (1951) were based on a quite different set of political conditions. They were intended to control Japan as well as to contain China and Russia; but, unlike NATO's inclusion of Germany in 1954, they did not look toward integrating Japan into a coherent regional coalition, and they contained no *mutual* defense obligations. The treaties give the United States the right to dispose its forces in and around Japan. They also contain clauses relating to Japan's internal security and the restraint of its foreign policy. American forces were originally authorized to put down disturbances in Japan that were instigated by outside powers, provided the Japanese government made an express request, but this authorization was dropped from the renewed security treaty in 1960. Japan was obligated to settle its international disputes amicably, and was pledged not to give bases to a third state. Although the 1960 revision relaxed the special constraints upon Japan, it still bore the marks of American tutelage.

The second set of post-Korean alliances, extending to Asian areas beyond the Pacific defense perimeter, included the Mutual Defense Treaty with Korea (1953), the Southeast Asia Collective Defense Treaty (1954), and the Mutual Defense Treaty with the Republic of China (1954). All these treaties, like those with the Philippines, Australia, and New Zealand, provide that the parties "separately and jointly, by means of continuous and effective self-help and mutual aid will maintain and develop their individual and collective capacity to resist armed attack." They define the *casus foederis* as an "armed attack," state that each party recognizes that an armed attack "would endanger its own peace and safety," and declare that each party will, in the event of an attack, act to meet the common danger "in accordance with its constitutional processes."

In recognition of the threat of indirect or internal aggression in Asia, the SEATO treaty obligates its members to consult on measures for common defense in the event of threats to the "inviolability or the integrity of the territory or the sovereignty or political independence" of any party, state, or territory covered by the treaty. The treaty with the Republic of China expresses the signatories' determination to resist "Communist subversive activities directed from without against their territorial integrity and political stability."

The treaties with Korea and China, like the one with Japan, authorize the United States to station armed forces in their territory. In what amounts to restraining clauses, these two treaties also define the covered areas in such a way as to make the treaties inoperative should these states seek to change the status quo by offensive military action. Another indication of the limited nature of the underlying political consensus is contained in an "understanding," issued by the United States prior to signing the SEATO treaty, that confines the *casus foederis* to communist aggression.

These Asian-Pacific alliances, as their terms suggest, were intended, first, to project American deterrent power against communist expansion and, second, to serve as political frameworks for building up local security forces, opposing internal threats, and restraining the foreign policies of allies. Compared to NATO, their relatively inexplicit and limited terms of obligation indicate a narrower and less substantial consensus among the signatories on the nature and importance of interests that would warrant considering the use of force. They reflect the fact that the nations in the area are relatively heterogeneous and unstable and have foreign policies that are rather inchoate and in flux. They also reflect the fact that in American eyes the area does not approach the material, political, and cultural importance of Europe. But of more substantive importance than the difference in terms is the fact that, unlike NATO, the Asian-Pacific treaties have not been implemented by organizations that establish American local forces under United States command on local territory in peacetime.

In formal outline SEATO is a multilateral regional alliance like NATO; but, as its principal architect, Secretary of State Dulles, recognized, it is not based on anything like the kind of regional cohesion, political stability, or military po-

tential that underlies NATO.[3] Nor is it a full-fledged organization (for which reason Dulles preferred to have the treaty
called by its proper name). Under both SEATO and the
ANZUS pact there have been collective military planning
and exercises but no effort to establish integrated forces
under central command.[4]

The political-military consensus in SEATO was always
quite limited. Almost from SEATO's inception, France and
Britain were more interested in other parts of the world and
generally opposed any move toward action by other members. Britain's forthcoming withdrawal from military positions "East of Suez," signaled in the Defense White Paper of
1967, will remove the one great friendly power in the area
that could supplement America's military and political presence. Australia might gradually assume a larger role in the
ocean areas to the north of it, but it has neither the resources nor the historic ties to project its power to the mainland. The Philippines, Thailand, and Pakistan were included partly to give the treaty the sanction of Asian
membership. Yet the ties of interest among these states are

3. In testifying in behalf of the Southeast Asia Collective Defense
Treaty, Dulles emphasized three differences between it and NATO:
(1) It did not contemplate building up a local joint military force
and organization but relied instead on "the deterrent of our mobile
striking power." To duplicate the NATO pattern, he said, "would
require a diversion and commitment of strength which we do not
think is either practical or desirable or necessary." (2) It included a
provision to deal with subversion. (3) Its defense obligation was explicitly based, like the other Pacific pacts, on the "Monroe Doctrine
formula," which was somewhat less automatic than the obligation in
the North Atlantic Treaty.

4. SEATO has a small permanent staff and common budget. Its
principal military body is the Military Advisers, which is essentially a
biannual meeting of top military representatives with commands in
the area. ANZUS provides for consultations among military staffs and
foreign ministers.

extremely thin or nonexistent, and their ability to assist each
other is negligible. For the Asian members, SEATO consti-
tuted a channel and claim for preferential economic assistance but not a significant instrument of military security,
apart from its formalization of the American commitment.
Pakistan's membership, for all practical purposes, adds nothing to its bilateral links with the United States. Its subsequent rapprochement with China, marked by an agreement
with China concerning border areas in dispute between
Pakistan, India, and China, amounted to virtual defection
from the alliance.[5] France's independent course in Southeast
Asia, under De Gaulle and during the Vietnam war, leads in
the same direction.

3. *The Middle East*

Similar in conception to these Asian treaties were
America's post-Korean War ties to states in the Middle East
through the Baghdad Pact (1955), which the United States
helped create in order to close a gap in the line of deterrence from SEATO to NATO. But it seems that Dulles also
expected the regional members of a Middle Eastern pact to
add something substantial to local military power. With this
latter purpose in mind, he first joined Britain, France, and
Turkey in trying to induce the Arab states to participate in
a Middle East Defense Command. When Egypt refused thus
to subordinate its regional interests to a cold war alliance
directed against Russia, in which Iraq would have had a

5. In 1962 the United States gave military assistance to India in its
border clash with China without making any stipulations about settling the Kashmir dispute with Pakistan. Thereupon Pakistan's turn
toward China, which had begun with the accession of the pro-Chinese
Foreign Minister Bhutto in 1960, became pronounced. The United
States suspension of military and economic assistance to both Pakistan
and India in their Kashmir fight of 1965 further alienated Pakistan
from alignment with the United States. Pakistan may continue to
retain ties to the United States and, formally, to SEATO and CENTO,
but it also seems eager to cultivate ties with Moscow as well as Peking.

more important role, Dulles turned his efforts to the "northern tier"—the most cohesive group of states in the Middle East—and engineered the Baghdad Pact. Egypt soon became the principal client of the Soviet Union in the Middle East.[6] This pact, signed in 1955 by Iraq (which defected in 1958) and Turkey, and soon afterward by the United Kingdom, Pakistan, and Iran, has a rudimentary organization for military and political consultation which entitles it to be called the Central Treaty Organization, or CENTO. However, without the paramountcy of American power, it lacks the necessary ingredient that makes SEATO a working collective defense alliance.

In the Middle East, as in Southeast Asia, the United States was eager to convey the impression of regional initiative and consent, but it was reluctant to be a full participant in an alliance, partly because it had greater confidence in the allies' ability to organize a common defense and partly because it was more sensitive to regional distaste for a pro-Western alliance. Therefore the United States refrained from joining CENTO, although it has since participated in several key committees, and it has made what are, in effect, bilateral alliances with Iran, Pakistan, and Turkey, which became effective in 1959. The operative clause of these agreements reads,

> The Government of _____ is determined to resist aggression. In case of aggression against _____, the Government of the United States of America, in accordance with the Constitution of the United States of America, will take such appropriate action, including the use of armed forces, as may be mutually agreed upon and as is envisaged in the Joint Resolution [that is, the so-called

6. By the end of 1966, according to Walter Laqueur, "Soviet bloc arms deliveries to Egypt were estimated at between $1.5 and $2 billion —including virtually the whole Egyptian Air Force, more than a thousand tanks, much of its navy, ten thousand trucks, and other equipment." *The Reporter,* June 29, 1967, p. 18.

Middle East Resolution] to promote Peace and Stability in the Middle East, in order to assist the Government of _____ at its request.

These agreements, although much hedged about, project some calculable probability of military involvement by the United States in extreme circumstances. They are probably more important for deterrence than CENTO, where the divergencies of interest among the northern tier states constitute as big an obstacle to collective cohesion as do the divergencies among SEATO's members. CENTO is no.more relevant to Pakistan's principal concern, the conflict with India, than SEATO. Iran finds the alliance irrelevant to its growing anxiety concerning pressures from Egypt and increasingly looks to the Soviet Union for support.[7] The alliance is equally irrelevant to Turkey's most immediate concern, its antagonism with Greece over Cyprus.

Meanwhile, the Soviet Union, taking advantage of the erosion of United States ties with the Middle East, has steadily capitalized upon indigenous rivalries, the selective use of military assistance, the desire of CENTO members to demonstrate their independence of American influence, and the Arabian animosity toward Israel (which is supported materially and politically principally by the United States) in order to seek political primacy among at least the revisionist Middle Eastern states. In some measure, it has succeeded in

7. Iran is concerned that, when the British leave Aden and South Arabia in 1968, Nasser's Egypt will become the major power in the area, leaving the Shah face to face with his bitterest enemy across the Persian Gulf. Against this danger Soviet support is far more relevant than CENTO with its emphasis upon pressure exerted from the north. In February, 1967, the U.S.S.R. gave Iran $90,000,000 worth of military equipment in exchange for Iranian natural gas. Pakistan was reported to have entered into a similar arrangement. The flexibility of military assistance agreements and the complexity of Middle Eastern alignments are illustrated by the fact that the Soviet Union has been the primary supporter of Egypt since Soviet bloc arms shipments to that country began in 1955.

this objective while presenting itself, in contrast to Western states, as a disinterested supporter of nonalignment in the area, with no oil concessions or other special interests.

Clearly, the Middle Eastern pacts of the United States—indeed, all its post-Korean alliances combined—despite their geographical scope and overlapping membership, do not comprise a tightly knit system of alliances or, indeed, any system at all. Rather, they are an aggregation of disparate, formalized, special relationships that have no linkage other than their common purpose to clarify and sanction the projection of American deterrent power along the periphery of Eurasia and to provide the political framework for fostering indigenous local resistance to communist penetration in a highly diversified, fragmented, and rapidly changing environment inhabited by weak states.

4. *Africa*

The essential determinants of effective alliance with the United States—or with any other state—are even weaker in Africa. There the inchoate, evanescent nature of international politics in the less-developed areas is especially marked among the dozens of new states that have recently made the transition from colonial status to independence. Most of these states are weaker militarily and more unstable internally than those in Asia and the Middle East. Across the often poorly established and ill-defined boundaries of nominal states, personal, ethnic, and tribal conflicts and alignments may be more significant than ostensibly international politics.

The cold war has touched Africa, as everywhere. In the Congo civil war of 1960-63, it led to limited but crucial American intervention, to much more limited but indecisive Soviet intervention, and to the deployment of a force sponsored by the United Nations. Africa south of the Sahara seems to be ripe for internal and boundary wars. Endemic violence and unrest, together with recent colonial experience and racial resentment, make the area vulnerable to communist penetration. Yet, as elsewhere in the world, the Soviet or Chinese capacity to gain control of even the weakest countries not adjacent to them has thus far proved to be very limited.[8] Moreover, their efforts have set up countervailing tendencies in Africa, where military leaders have taken control of a number of countries.

In addition to these features of the African environment that militate against the creation of alliances, it should be noted that the acceleration of nationalism and the intensification of the cold war in Africa that followed the attainment of national independence took place after the period of American alliance-building in the 1950's. By that time the United States had lost its original enthusiasm for alliances and had adopted a hopeful view of nonalignment. So the United States was no more alliance-minded than the indigenous states.

Consequently the United States has not tried to build a network of alliances in Africa. Strictly speaking, its only alliance is a defense treaty with Liberia. Britain's only remaining defense agreement in Africa is with Libya. France has eleven defense agreements with former French colonies. However, all the African alliances with external powers are essentially aimed at internal security and control. For this purpose, as well as for obtaining military facilities, the many base and military assistance agreements, in which the United States is a major participant along with France, the United Kingdom, Belgium, Italy, Russia, and China, are far more consequential.

5. *Nonalignment*

The role of alliances in American foreign policy outside Europe has been further limited by the strong appeal of

8. It remains to be seen whether the controlling position of communist parties in Congo Brazzaville and Zanzibar is a model for other places.

nonalignment; that is, the policy of avoiding alliance with, or strong dependence upon, either side in the cold war. This appeal is based partly on the normal desire of states anywhere to avoid the involvements, restraints, risks, costs, and other liabilities of an alliance if their security does not seem to require one. Along the periphery of Eurasia, fear of a Chinese or Soviet military threat has been largely confined to nations that are adjacent to these great powers and that have had bitter experience fighting communists; but even some of these states (for example, India) calculate that they are spared the need of alliance by the over-all military balance and by a kind of tacit alliance with the United States, or the Soviet Union, or both.

Another appeal of nonalignment stems from the desire to receive economic and other benefits from both sides and thereby take advantage of American-Soviet (and, more recently, Sino-Soviet) competition for favor and influence in the so-called Third World.

Nonalignment reflects the tendency of the new and weak states to be far more concerned with their internal problems, and in some cases with local conflicts and rivalries, than with the cold war, which they view as a distraction. They would like the dominant currents of international politics to revolve around the issues of anticolonialism (or antineocolonialism) and economic development rather than around the power competition between communist and noncommunist states. If they join an alliance under circumstances other than an imminent threat to their security, it is likely to be for the sake of gaining tangible great-power support in their contest with a local adversary, as in the case of Pakistan's joining SEATO to increase its power against India.

Yet nonalignment has been more than a calculated stratagem. Among states recently liberated from colonial rule, it has a mystique. It expresses the assertion of an independent foreign policy and the rejection of the power politics of the old and advanced states—an attitude akin to America's traditional rejection of alliances, except for overtones of anticolonialism. It is this mystique that underlies the claim of the nonaligned countries to be a positive and active force for peace. Accordingly, the United Nations General Assembly, where the smallest state has formal equality with the largest, is their preferred arena of international politics (although their actual division into voting blocs and their negligible influence in pacifying great-power disputes lends little substance to the claim). There they can combine the pursuit of special interests with the sense of being beneficent participants in world politics. They can enjoy some of the superficial satisfactions of an active foreign policy with maximum freedom from the hard responsibilities of power politics, including alliances.

The coincidence of intensified indigenous nationalism and nonalignment sentiment in the Third World with the American effort to reinforce deterrence on the Eurasian periphery by means of alliances created something of a contradiction between America's security policy and its desire to associate itself with the modernizing forces at work in what seemed to be an increasingly decisive arena of the cold war. In the mid-1950's the United States sometimes seemed to emphasize the first interest at the expense of the second. Thus Secretary Dulles, in a much-advertised remark in June, 1956, denounced neutralism as the fallacy that "a nation can buy safety for itself by being indifferent to the fate of others" and added that it "has increasingly become an obsolete conception and, except under very exceptional circumstances, it is an immoral and short-sighted conception."

It would be incorrect, however, to interpret Dulles' irritation with what he considered to be the self-righteous imprudence and irresponsibility of some of the new states as part of a policy of collecting as many allies among them as possible. If the American government ever envisioned creating a solid barrier of aligned states in Asia and the Middle East, it abandoned the project upon discovering the limited value of SEATO and the problems of extending American commitments in an area like the Middle East. It discovered that nonalignment covered a considerable variety of foreign policies that were not necessarily unfriendly to the United States and that, as manifestations of nationalism, might offer the most effective resistance to communist designs. It found itself competing with Soviet appeals to all the nationalist and idealistic sentiments associated with nonalignment. Therefore, as Afro-Asian states embraced nonalignment, the American government progressively came to terms with neutralist sentiment. One indication of this trend was Dulles' support of nonaligned states against two of America's major allies, Britain and France, during the Suez crisis of 1956 when the United States and the U.S.S.R. combined to oppose the "aggression" against Egypt. Although the Eisenhower administration did not actively court the nonaligned states, it did reach the conclusion that the capacity of new states for effective alliance is limited and that it is more important for them to be truly independent and devoted to their internal development and stability than to be aligned.

Under President Kennedy, the government made a more determined appeal to nationalist sentiment and pursued a calculated effort to stabilize competition with the Soviet Union in the Third World on a favorable basis, emphasizing the positive contribution that nonaligned states might make to international harmony and their own development. It identified American interests with a world of "diversity" in contrast to the communist view that the nonaligned states, like the others, must eventually be in one of two camps—socialist or capitalist. With the wariness of one chastened by experience, Secretary of State Rusk often remarked that the United States was not seeking any new allies.[9] In the midst

9. For example, in a television interview on December 23, 1965, Mr. Rusk said, "We're not out looking for more allies. We have quite enough, thank you, for the moment. We have over forty. They [the South Vietnamese] can be nonaligned. The problem is, can they be safe from aggression?" *Department of State Bulletin,* no. 1386, January 17, 1966.

of the Vietnam war President Johnson praised Burma's "jealously guarded neutrality" and identified the underlying desire of nonaligned states to develop independently as "a fundamental principle of United States policy."[10] By the mid-1960's, a number of developments had somewhat diminished the appeal of nonalignment. The United States and the U.S.S.R. ceased to compete with one another quite so ardently for the favor of the new nations. Both discovered the limits of economic and military assistance as instruments of influence and control. The new nations themselves discovered that limited alignments with one contestant or the other in the cold war did not necessarily compromise their independence or involve them in extraregional disputes and that, at the same time, such alignments might promote their security with respect to local rivals and, in the case of India and a few other Asian states, against the looming menace of Communist China. China's attack upon the Indian border, its nuclear program, and its revolutionary fanaticism raised apprehensions that could not be allayed by nonalignment. To India, China's aspirations seemed to be leading to a kind of dual alignment with Washington and Moscow against Peking. The accentuation of local conflicts turned the attention of new states to problems of security and status that could not be solved by the formulas of nonalignment, and it reinforced the tendency to look at nonalignment as just one among several expedients to be pursued according to particular circumstances rather than as a universal principle of foreign policy for postcolonial states. The Sino-Soviet split accentuated the division among nonaligned countries, that is, between the moderate states like Yugoslavia, India, and the former French African colonies and the militant leftist states like Mali, Guinea, and Algeria. The death of Nehru, the political eclipse of Sukarno and Nkrumah, and the uncertain success of Nasser as a leader of

10. Remarks on the occasion of General Ne Win's visit to Washington, September 8, 1966.

the Arab world largely silenced the charismatic spokesmen of nonalignment on the world stage and contributed to the devaluation of the mystique of nonalignment.

On the other hand, the declining appeal of nonalignment as a general principle of foreign policy among the new and underdeveloped states does not necessarily foreshadow a more important role for alliances in the international politics of the Third World. The utility of alliances there will depend on many factors other than disillusionment with nonalignment. The fact remains that very few states in the Third World have the incentives, the material and political capability, or the historic experience and traditions to enter into alliances with the superpowers—or, for that matter, with any other states. In the absence of the very special political and military conditions that have fostered alliances among the advanced states, formal alliances are likely to remain much less attractive than more limited kinds of commitments. Nevertheless, these other kinds of commitments are not so different from alliances as to conceal the ambiguity and growing irrelevance of the old postulates of nonalignment.

6. *Commitments Other Than Alliances*

Despite the superficial resemblance of America's post-Korean extension of alliances and its pre-Korean alliance policy, alliances on the Asian periphery and in Africa have played a much more limited role than in Europe and Latin America.

SEATO and CENTO, the two multilateral alliances in the area that bear the greatest superficial resemblance to NATO, have lacked the substance and vitality to grow and adjust. Indeed, CENTO might be said to have been stillborn, since it almost entirely lacked a consensus on major security interests among its members and was largely irrelevant to some of their most vital concerns. SEATO represents a greater degree of common security interests among its members but, in practice, Pakistan and France have such divergent political interests from the rest that they do no` agree about the means of implementing the alliance. SEATO has served a limited function in facilitating some joint military planning and operations and in formalizing the American military presence in the area, but its multilateral form adds nothing essential to what is actually a set of bilateral arrangements with the United States. The chief value of its formal multilateral structure is to recruit indigenous Asian support, but it scarcely conceals American preponderance.

Therefore America's alliances in Asia, the Middle East, and Africa indicate far less about the real nature and extent of American military commitments than NATO indicated in Europe. They are much less significant than the network of commitments other than alliances in the area. Notable among these commitments are the many air, sea, and land bases and bilateral agreements under the military assistance program. Although these commitments generally entail more limited obligations than alliances do, they may also carry the implication of diplomatic and, in some cases, military co-operation; they serve many of the same functions as alliances.[11]

The chief function of bases is obvious—to enhance the military strength of the United States and, especially in the case of mainland bases, the credibility of its being used. Base agreements generally require a lesser order of co-operation and commitment from the host state than alliances do. Yet, because they provide direct assistance to the West and make

11. A complete description and interpretation of military assistance and base agreements between countries in the Third World and the advanced states—including those with the U.S.S.R., China, the United Kingdom, France, West Germany, and Italy—would show an elaborate network of alignments, many of which overlap. In this section, however, we must confine our sketch to the commitments of the United States.

the host a target, and because the communists have waged a continual propaganda campaign against them, nations not allied with the United States and directly threatened by the Soviet Union or China are reluctant to grant bases and to continue existing ones. Even where the United States enjoys a close alliance and mutual security interests, as in the case of its base on Okinawa (in which Japan has "residual sovereignty"), it may be under irresistible pressure to accept militarily disadvantageous restrictions upon its use of the base. The growth of indigenous nationalism and the increasing range and power of Soviet nuclear weapons have accentuated the pressures limiting American access to bases. China's growing nuclear power can be expected to have the same effect. These pressures are also reflected in the growing tendency of states to restrict or deny overflight rights. Although technological changes reduce the United States need for some kinds of bases (notably, bomber and missile bases), it still needs a number of them (especially staging bases for limited war operations); as some bases are phased out, it needs the remaining ones more than ever.

Military assistance agreements, by providing training and matériel, perform a variety of functions more nearly comparable to alliances. Their versatility is suggested by the fact that in recent years the United States has maintained them with over sixty countries. Their principal function (apart from supporting the military base program) is to strengthen local forces against external and internal communist threats, a function reflected in the allocation of about two-thirds of American military aid to eleven countries adjacent to or near the Soviet Union and China.[12] But some agreements are intended principally to provide access to a local government or military establishment and to deny access to other

12. According to a Department of Defense analysis, the flow of American arms to underdeveloped countries (not including the special cases of Greece, Turkey, South Vietnam, and South Korea) more than doubled from 1961 to 1967, rising to nearly $900 million in the fiscal

potential donors. Others are intended, like much economic aid, to support a friendly regime, to win favor in the nation being helped, or to enhance the power and status of a country or of particular groups within the country for a variety of other political purposes.

Military assistance agreements generally include a provision that states, in effect, that assistance shall be used only for the purposes of mutual interest for which it was given, but these purposes are not usually specified in the agreement.[13] Such agreements do not restrict the recipient's freedom of military action and diplomatic position by explicit or tacit obligations nearly as much as alliances do. Usually, the parties merely agree to co-operate for their security and defense. Consequently, military assistance agreements have

---

year ending June 30, 1967. The major reason for the increase was America's effort to offset the effects of increased Soviet arms shipments, which were estimated to be running at $500 million to $600 million annually. The Soviet Union was reported to have provided $4 billion to $5 billion worth of arms to noncommunist countries in the Third World since 1955, when its first big arms agreement was made with Egypt through Czechoslovakia. *New York Times,* September 5, 1967, p. 1; October 26, 1967, p. 11.

13. In the American agreement with Iran, for example, Iran "undertakes to utilize such military and economic assistance as may be provided by the government of the United States of America in the manner consonant with the aims and purposes set forth by the governments associated in the Declaration signed at London on July 28, 1958." This declaration, signed by the United States, Iran, Pakistan, Turkey, and the United Kingdom, simply reaffirmed the determination of these members of the Baghdad Pact "to maintain their collective security and to resist aggression, direct or indirect" and "to strengthen further their united defense posture in the area." The principal purpose of the kind of generalized restriction on the utilization of military assistance incorporated in the agreement with Iran is to satisfy the requirements of American legislation authorizing the assistance (in this case the Mutual Assistance Act of 1954) that United States weapons and equipment will not be transferred to or employed against local states in accordance with the special interests of the recipient rather than the donor.

some of the flexibility that alliances used to have before the age of popular governments and nuclear deterrence. Thus, many nonaligned states have been willing to accept military aid from either West or East. Some, like India and Indonesia, have received aid from both sides simultaneously. Pakistan, although an American ally, receives military aid from the Soviet Union. The United States has given about $800 million of aid to Yugoslavia's armed forces to support its independent and once heretical position among communist states. It continued to give modest military assistance to Indonesia in order to retain access to its military establishment while that country was approaching the Chinese camp and pursuing local territorial ambitions against Britain and Malaysia.

Despite their flexibility, however, military assistance agreements can exert great tangible political effects, since they may visibly change the local balance of power, introduce foreign advisers into a country, and establish a technical dependency upon the donor. The Soviet arms agreement with Egypt and the American military assistance agreement with Pakistan are cases in point.

Of course, military assistance agreements may be supplements (as with Pakistan) rather than alternatives to alliances. Indeed, the great proportion of military assistance has gone to allies. In the Middle East it was apparently not only a by-product but also a lever of alliance for the United States.

In addition to base and military assistance agreements, America's commitments depend heavily on unilateral declarations, like the Truman Doctrine, that implicitly or explicitly convey intent to use force in certain kinds of contingencies. For example, the Middle East Resolution of 1957, which announced the so-called Eisenhower Doctrine, declared that the United States "regards as vital to the national interest and world peace the preservation of the independence and integrity of the nations of the Middle East," and that the President may "use armed force to assist any nation or group of nations requesting assistance against armed aggression from any country controlled by international communism." In accordance with this resolution, American troops landed in Lebanon in 1958 at the request of that government, even though the immediate objective was not to fight aggression but merely to stabilize potentially explosive local conflicts among the states in the area.[14]

There are counterparts of the Truman Doctrine and the Middle East Resolution in unilateral declarations concerning particular countries and surrounding areas. For example, as a supplement to the defense treaty with the Republic of China, the Congress of the United States adopted a joint resolution in January, 1955, authorizing the President "to employ the armed forces of the United States as he deems necessary for the specific purpose of securing and protecting Formosa and the Pescadores against armed attack, this authority to include the securing and protection of such related positions and territories of that area now in friendly hands and the taking of such other measures as he judges to be required or appropriate in assuring the defense of Formosa and the Pescadores."

During the Quemoy and Matsu crisis of 1958, President Eisenhower and Secretary of State Dulles made statements warning Peking that China's belligerent actions in the Straits made the protection of Quemoy and Matsu increasingly vital to the defense of Taiwan and that a major assault on the offshore islands would fall under the Congressional resolution.

In September, 1962, during the Cuban missile crisis, President Kennedy declared, "If at any time the Communist buildup in Cuba were to endanger or interfere with our

14. In an earlier agreement intended to stabilize Middle Eastern borders, the United States, the United Kingdom, and France signed a tripartite declaration in 1950 pledging "unalterable opposition to the use of force or threat of force between any of the states" in the area.

security in any way, including our base at Guantanamo, our passage to the Panama Canal, our missile and space activities at Cape Canaveral, or the lives of American citizens in this country, or if Cuba should ever attempt to export its aggressive purposes by force or the threat of force against any nation in this hemisphere, or become an offensive military base of significant capacity for the Soviet Union, then this country will do whatever must be done to protect its own security and that of its allies." A Congressional joint resolution of October 3, 1962, reinforced this declaration in similar language.

In May, 1965, during the Dominican crisis, President Johnson generalized this commitment in his declaration that "the American nations cannot, must not, and will not permit the establishment of another Communist government in the Western Hemisphere."

Such unilateral commitments, of course, need not be communicated publicly. At the height of Indonesia's guerrilla attacks in Borneo in 1963, the United States government, according to many reports in Washington, privately informed Sukarno that if the integrity and independence of Malaya were seriously threatened by his campaign of armed "confrontation," the United States would back up Commonwealth forces (which were obligated to assist Malaysia) with all the power of the Seventh Fleet. Assurances, as well as threats, may be communicated discreetly with little or no publicity. When Nasser blockaded the Gulf of Aqaba in 1967, American and Israeli officials cited an *aide-mémoire* given by Secretary of State Dulles to Ambassador Eban on February 11, 1957, declaring that the gulf "comprehends international waters, and that no nation has the right to prevent free and innocent passage in the gulf and through the straits giving access thereto."

For obvious reasons wars offer special occasions for extending commitments by declaration. Thus in August, 1964, following the Gulf of Tonkin incident in the Vietnam war,

Congress declared in response to President Johnson's request, "The United States regards as vital to its national interest and to world peace the maintenance of peace and security in Southeast Asia . . . the United States is, therefore, prepared, as the President determines, to take all necessary steps, including the use of armed force, to assist any member or protocol state of the Southeast Asia Collective Defense Treaty requesting assistance in defense of its freedom."

Such declarations, when applied to the protection of a specific state and made jointly with a representative of that state, can be tantamount to an alliance. A case in point is the joint declaration issued during the Laotian crisis in March, 1962, by Secretary of State Rusk and the Foreign Minister of Thailand to reinforce the commitment under SEATO to help Thailand in the event of "Communist armed attack" and to make this obligation "individual as well as collective." This commitment to defend Thailand without the approval of other SEATO signatories is reinforced by the development of large base installations and substantial military assistance, which includes American armed forces. A formal United States–Thailand alliance could scarcely create a more binding commitment. For that matter, the whole series of measures by which the United States extended its involvement in defending the government of South Vietnam illustrates strikingly the scope of commitments that can be incurred without a formal alliance.

Serving a function similar to unilateral declarations of military intent with respect to particular regions, countries, and locales are countless public statements about American military strategy. These are intended to convey the determination of the United States to respond militarily in a particular way to particular kinds of contingencies in particular areas of the world. One can match these statements with similar ones by the Soviet government, although Soviet strategic pronouncements, like Soviet declarations of intent with respect to particular areas, countries, and incidents, tend to be less specific.

7. *Indigenous Alliances*

So far, most military commitments in the Third World, whether made by alliances or other means, have been organized under the preponderant influence of the United States and the Soviet Union. America's official rhetoric of partnership and interdependence cannot conceal this manifestation of a generally bipolar world. The American government customarily hails its multilateral alliances as interdependent parts of a regional security system; but actually, since all are to some degree extensions of American power, each one adapted to unique conditions and having little to do with the others, they are quite a departure from the vision of a world of self-sustaining regional alliances that Americans held earlier in the cold war. This vision looked forward to multilateral alliances that would blunt national separatism while concerting power and would relieve the United States from military burdens while fostering harmony among self-reliant collectivities.

Since the demanding ideal of self-sustaining regional organizations has not materialized even among the economically advanced and politically mature states of Europe, it is no wonder that it has failed to materialize outside Europe. Yet in the course of adjusting to the conditions of national independence, the fledgling states of the Third World have formed a number of regional organizations for largely non-military co-operation. Several of these resemble indigenous alliances in some respects. A few—particularly in Southeast Asia—might even lay the political foundations of genuine alliances. In the least economically and politically developed areas (like Africa south of the Sahara), however, autonomous security arrangements are less apt to grow out of efforts toward regional co-operation and security than out of

the consolidation of a pattern of local conflicts and alignments, resulting in mutually restraining balances of power.
Through such local balances of power, the superpowers and
perhaps some of the second-rank, former colonial powers
might gain access to the politics of the Third World that
would be more effective, yet more indirect, than at present.
Such alliances might enable the United States to support at
least a minimal degree of order at a tolerable level of involvement by giving marginal assistance to local states rather
than by acting as the preponderant power in the area.

Latin America appears to be the area in which indigenous
alliances are least likely to develop. The most obvious obstacles to them are the operation of the existing regional
system, the fact that in this system the United States handles
the military power directed against external aggression, that
United States–Latin-American relations rather than intraregional relations predominate, and that collective co-
operation takes precedence over the interests of special
blocs.[15] Although the strong movement toward *afirmación
nacional* has enlivened the endemic drive of Latin-American
states to be economically, politically, and culturally independent of the United States and has placed strict limits on
a more intensive development of the OAS as a collective
security organization, it has not encouraged the development
of separate alliances. Instead, it has led to a kind of pan-
Latin-American nationalism, manifested in the movement
for a Latin-American Free Trade Area (LAFTA) and a
Latin-American Parliament, which might give Latin-
American countries greater leverage in their negotiations
with the United States on matters of common interest to
them. Whether their interests are sufficiently common and
compelling to lead to effective regional institutions remains

15. Thus the representatives of Chile, Colombia, Ecuador, Peru, and
Venezuela who met in Bogotá in August, 1966, took pains to deny that
they were forming any bloc that would obstruct the closer integration
of all the Latin-American countries.

in doubt, but, in any case, no one claims that these institutions would be the precursors of an autonomous alliance.

In Asia there has been a plethora of proposals for regional co-operation for twenty years. Yet local conflicts in the area have grown along with interest in regional co-operation. These conflicts include animosities with deep ethnic and cultural roots (as between Cambodia and her neighbors, Thailand and both Vietnams, or between Pakistan and India), newer and possibly ephemeral conflicts of territorial interest (as between the Philippines and Malaysia over North Borneo), and combinations of both (as between Indonesia and Malaysia).

Despite these divisive influences, however, several Asian organizations of economic, cultural, and broadly political co-operation have been created: the Association for Southeast Asia (ASA), established by the Philippines, Malaya, and Thailand in 1961; Maphilindo, created by Malaysia, the Philippines, and Indonesia in 1963; the Asian Development Bank, set up in 1966, with Japan matching the capital contribution of the United States; ECAFE, the United Nations economic commission in the region; and the Asian and Pacific Council (ASPAC), formed in 1966 by a conference of nine countries at Seoul. Yet these organizations are most successful when they are directed toward widely shared economic goals. Neither their composition nor their organizing purpose is suitable for mobilizing power for common security. When concrete political issues come into play among their members, such issues are likely to be either divisive or else too ephemeral to sustain co-operation. Thus ASA was seriously weakened in 1963 when the Philippines laid claim to North Borneo (now Sabah, a Malaysian state). Maphilindo was based largely on a convergence of the acquisitive aims of the Philippines and Indonesia in Borneo, but the demise of Sukarno undermined this convergence.

The establishment of the Association of Southeast Asian Nations (ASEAN) by Indonesia, Malaysia, Thailand, the

Philippines, and Singapore in August, 1967, may be more significant, since it is based on a new consciousness of the need for common security arrangements against Chinese and Chinese-supported incursions in the area, and since it has the indispensable participation of Indonesia. ASEAN, representing a subregional group of states with a population of 18,000,000, could undertake not only the economic co-operation in which ASA is engaged but also military and technical co-operation against subversion and guerrilla warfare. But ASEAN is now a long way from organizing itself for any kind of military co-operation and is far from subordinating the latent divergent interests of its members to a consensus upon anything so basic and controversial as a tangible security policy.

The only Asian state with significant capacity to project its own military power and organize an alignment of power with other East Asian states in the foreseeable future is Japan. India, in its growing fear of China, is quickly losing its inhibitions against *Grosspolitik,* but it is too weak internally, and it lacks the basic affinities with other Asian states to enable it to lead an alliance. In time, Japan's rediscovery of extensive political and economic interests in Southeast Asia, its resurgent nationalism, its desire to diminish its dependence on the United States, and its apprehensions about China's growing nuclear force may combine to induce the nation to play a major role in Asian power politics. If so, Japan would readily become an equal component in a multipolar balance of power, along with the United States, China, and Russia. But this is a distant and cloudy prospect. Japan, in the aftermath of World War II, is still self-consciously a nonmilitary state so far as any objective beyond its own self-defense is concerned; and, if it were to abandon this constraint, its rising influence in Asia as a leader of economic and broad political co-operation might soon be replaced by Asian fear and antipathy.

The Middle East, even more markedly than Asia, is fragmented by persistent divisions and antagonisms. It lacks states that are capable of organizing a regional alliance by dint of superior power and ability to hold the confidence and trust of neighboring states. In political orientation the area is fragmented not only by Arab-Israeli hostility, but also by divisions among the Arab states. One basic division is between the Arab Middle East (which itself is divided into the states of the fertile crescent, the Arabian peninsula, the Nile Valley, and other lands west of Egypt) and the northern tier (Turkey, Iran, Afghanistan, and Pakistan). Overlying these divisions is a cleavage between professedly revolutionary or socialist states (Egypt, Syria, Iraq, and Algeria) and conservative monarchies (Saudi Arabia, Jordan, Libya, and, on some issues, Morocco), which contest control of marginal portions of the Arabian peninsula, where the United Kingdom has granted independence to the Federation of South Arabia. This cleavage and the geographical divisions are, in turn, crisscrossed by other conflicts and alignments from time to time, such as the rivalry between Egypt and Iraq. Only when events occasionally conspire to focus animosities against Israel is there anything like regional solidarity in the area.

Indigenous alliances, strictly defined, do not play an important role in the complicated, shifting pattern of Middle Eastern alignment. Nevertheless, intraregional alignments are somewhat more substantial than in other parts of the Afro-Asian area. They are based on a more intensive and protracted interaction between governments. Moreover, the Arab League, although by no means an operating security organization, comes closer to performing the functions of a regional alliance than any other purely indigenous multilateral organization in the Third World.

The Treaty of Saadabad (1937), still technically in force, engages Turkey, Iran, Afghanistan, and Iraq to consult about threats to their common interests that may be posed by an international conflict, but it is of negligible importance, having outlived the immediate prospect of the contingency it was intended to meet—the creation of a Kurdish national state—and having been superseded, for other purposes, by the Baghdad Pact. Algeria, Morocco, and Egypt aligned with the so-called Casablanca group of African states, which was organized in January, 1961, to pursue nonalignment on a continental basis and to create (but only on paper) a joint military command. Libya and Tunisia initially aligned with a parallel combination of African states, the Monrovia group, in May, 1961, but later withdrew because of the omission of Algeria. Algeria, Sudan, and Egypt joined the Organization for African Unity (OAU), which was founded in May, 1963, and subsumed both the Casablanca and Monrovia groups. Algeria, Morocco, Tunisia, and Libya from time to time have discussed a project for a Maghreb Federation, but the project seems incapable of surmounting diversities of political orientation among its members. Tunisia has sponsored a combination of states formerly associated with France. Egypt and Sudan have discussed an alignment based on their association as states of the Nile Valley. But none of these proposals or undertakings is as substantial as various moves toward union among the socialist Arab states, such as the abortive United Arab Republic, which united Egypt and Syria from 1959 to 1961, and the subsequent efforts toward a tripartite union to include Iraq. If such an amalgamation were to persist—which is doubtful—it might lead to a countervailing association of conservative states, as represented by Saudi Arabia's proposal of an Islamic League, which would include Iran, possibly Morocco, and also perhaps Tunisia, loosely aligned in opposition to Egypt. Yet these conjectural groupings are improbable.

In form, the League of Arab States overshadows any of these projects. The League was organized during World War II by the then independent Arab states, and it now includes all predominantly Arab areas except the enclaves of lingering British authority and influence along the Arabian littoral. It provides for the establishment of unified policies with respect to a broad range of concerns. It also pledges its members to "respect the form of government obtaining in other states of the League . . . and . . . not to take any action tending to change that form" and also to function as a collective security organization in dealing with disputes among members. By the terms of the Joint Defense and Economic Treaty of 1950, the League's members are obliged to consider an act of aggression against any member as aggression against all. This treaty provides for a council of representatives from all states, supported by a permanent secretariat headed by an elected secretary general and a staff drawn from all Arab states. The council has an elaborate set of committees, but the principal auxiliary bodies are the economic council and the joint defense council. The latter is charged with planning and co-ordinating functions similar to those of SHAPE in NATO, although the establishment of a unified command is reserved until the onset of hostilities.

In actuality, however, the Arab League has failed to achieve any integration of policy and administration except, occasionally, in opposition to Israel.[16] Even in economic integration, the League's provisions have little reality because the Arab states, in the main, are not complementary to one another as markets and producing areas. More than the countries of Southeast Asia or South America, the Middle Eastern states depend for their economic welfare and progress on the industrial systems of the outside world.

In Africa international political activity is characterized on the one hand by the intensification of national conflicts among new states still seeking national identities and on the

16. Even then, it is noteworthy that before the Arab-Israeli war of June, 1967, Egypt and Jordan, on the one hand, and Jordan and Iraq, on the other, found it necessary to sign mutual defense treaties to perform the functions that the instrumentalities of the League were supposed to perform.

other hand by efforts toward pan-African organizations to foster broad co-operation and harmony. In general, the new states of Africa have neither the military capacity, the political stability, nor the traditional political relationships among themselves to have developed distinct, enduring patterns of alignment, let alone indigenous alliances. There have been alignments of some political significance—Mali and Guinea, Ghana and Guinea, the 1960 Union of African States, the 1961 Casablanca Group, and the conservative, French-speaking Conseil d'Entente—but they have had no military importance.

The only alliances that have been formed have resulted from military confrontations of some duration. In July, 1963, Kenya and Ethiopia signed a pact for consultation in event of an attack on either, based on their common interest in resisting Somalia's incursions and territorial claims in the area. The guerrilla warfare against the Portuguese in Angola, Guinea, and Mozambique since 1961 has received financial, material, and training assistance from African countries acting unilaterally, collectively, and as pipelines for military assistance from outside Africa. In effect the Liberation Committee of the OAU acts as a coalition against colonialism and white minority rule. In reality the ineffective, sporadic, and largely unco-ordinated military assistance provided shows that the OAU is less of an alliance than the Arab League.

The OAU, established in May, 1963, was a merger of several African groupings: the Union of African States, the Casablanca Group, the Brazzaville Group, the Monrovia-Lagos Group, and PAFMECSA (Pan-African Freedom Movement of East, Central and Southern Africa). It did not incorporate these shifting coalitions so much as it papered over the cracks in African unity, which reappear whenever the OAU tries to make a firm commitment on controversial issues. Consequently, as a peacekeeping organization the OAU can, at most, sanction *ad hoc* operations undertaken by its members, as it endorsed Tanganyika's military aid request to Ethiopia and Nigeria (both of which sent limited armed forces) to replace British troops, which had restored order against army mutinies in Kenya, Uganda, and Tanganyika early in 1964. It is more promising in the field of pacific settlement where it has already helped arrange mediations of border disputes and where it provides a forum for a growing opposition on the part of some states to subversion by others. Essentially, however, the OAU is an organizational expression of several objectives that it is incapable of implementing with joint action—independence from European control, liberation of the remaining colonial areas, stabilization of the territorial order inherited from Europe, and outlawry of subversion and coups as instruments of foreign policy.

I conclude that there is little prospect of the emergence in the next decade or two of regional or subregional balances of power and systems of order—or disorder—based on indigenous alliances among the underdeveloped states. Regional organizations like ASEAN and the OAU may provide useful international political experience to new states and somewhat dampen intraregional tensions, but they cannot perform the peacekeeping or collective security functions of the OAS, and they show little promise of acting as significant constraints against external aggression. The only indigenous regional grouping that comes close to performing the military functions of an alliance is the Arab League, which finds its sole source of cohesion in opposition to Israel.

The development of genuine alliance systems in the Third World probably depends on the emergence of a more highly structured configuration of power and interests through accentuation of a regional threat by China or the Soviet Union; the intensification and clarification of intraregional conflicts; the emergence of strong states with regional or subregional primacy, capable of organizing a pattern of commitments embracing lesser states; and the development by presently weak countries of sufficient military capability and political stability to sustain effective military commitments. These conditions seem quite improbable and remote. In any event, the international tensions and conflicts accompanying them would probably be an ironic refutation of the American ideal of regionalism.

A more likely and probably less disruptive potential development in the Third World would take the form of loosely knit subregional alignments for economic and diplomatic co-operation and for rudimentary military co-operation (in weapons, matériel, intelligence, staff work, training, and the like). Such alignments might mitigate national dissensions, provide important resistance to low-level, quasi-internal military incursions, and serve as a multilateral medium for utilizing countervailing external assistance against military-political pressure from a major power outside the area.

8. *Sino-Soviet Alliance and Schism*

In the Third World, as in Europe, the role of alliances in United States policy has been primarily a product of United States–Soviet competition, and to a lesser degree of United States–Chinese conflict, that arose when Soviet and Chinese policies were thought to be two sides of the same communist coin, minted in the Sino-Soviet alliance of 1950. Perhaps the United States would eventually have extended its commitments in the Third World, even if there had been no communist expansionist efforts in the area, if only to seek a modicum of stability in an otherwise chaotic field of power. In fact, however, these commitments were principally applications of containment against communist incursions (especially during the Korean and Indochinese wars) which seemed to be instruments of Soviet and Chinese expansion. American commitments will continue to respond to the policies and actions of communist states with power in the area. But these policies have changed and diverged notably from the time they provided the initial impetus for the extension of American alliances. The breach in the Sino-Soviet alliance, which is both cause and effect of the divergence, is the single most important change in the structure of power and commitments since the establishment of NATO. Consequently, the future of alliances in the Third World, as elsewhere, is bound to be affected by the future of Sino-Soviet relations and its impact on the policies of these two states.

After the end of the Korean and Indochinese wars and the death of Stalin, both the Soviet Union and Communist China, for somewhat different reasons (the former being primarily interested in Europe, the latter in Asia), turned toward a less militant strategy. In the Third World the new strategy played down violent revolutionary activity and concentrated on associating communist states and parties with local aspirations for national independence and modernization, often in support of noncommunist parties and governments at the expense of local communists. The Russians and Chinese ceased to condemn noncommunist nonaligned states, like India and Indonesia, as lackeys of imperialism. Instead they appealed to the sentiments and interests associated with nonalignment in an effort to hasten the erosion of Western influence, counteract America's projection of power in the area, and ultimately attach the new states to the socialist camp. The Bandung Conference of 1955 (to which the Soviet Union was not invited) dramatized this strategy in Asia, as the Geneva Conference of 1955 celebrated the "spirit of Geneva" in the West. Khrushchev and Bulganin launched Moscow's version of the Bandung strategy by visits to India, Burma, Indonesia, and other capitals in the Third World, scattering promises of economic and military assistance as they went.

In 1957-58, however, China turned to a more militant posture, marked by the occupation of Tibet and the incitement of crises in the Straits of Formosa, on the Indian border, and in Laos. The shift toward militancy came partly in response to the Soviet sputnik propaganda victory and the concomitant campaign to convey the impression that the world balance of power had shifted toward the communist bloc. But the Soviet attempt to capitalize on its technological advances in order to improve its position in Europe, as in the Berlin crisis of 1958-61, and its effort to expand its influence in the Middle East and the Congo were not matched by any enthusiasm for backing China's aggressive policies in Asia. Moreover, Soviet and Chinese appeals to neutralist sentiment in Asia, as well as their relations with communist parties in the area, became increasingly competitive. The strategies of the two allies diverged increasingly, with the U.S.S.R. favoring a less risky strategy of "peaceful coexistence" aimed at gaining the favor of nationalist-neutralist states and China advocating the more militant course of encouraging revolutionary activity.

The numerous causes of the Sino-Soviet split include (1) the historically familiar contest for power and prestige between two ambitious nations of sufficiently equal strength to incite rivalry and sufficient independence from each other to permit active competition, (2) China's frustrating economic and military dependence on the Soviet Union, (3) the difference of national interests between two states in quite different geopolitical circumstances and stages of economic development, (4) the theocratic nature of the communist system, which admits only one truth and therefore only one authoritative interpreter, and (5) a difference of revolutionary experience expressed in divergent strategies and doctrines of revolution.

Among the numerous events that aggravated the schism, the Soviet unwillingness to back up China's pressure against the Nationalists in the Quemoy and Matsu crisis of 1958 with unqualified threats of Soviet nuclear support against the United States, and the Soviet failure to continue helping the construction of China's nuclear force after 1959 were especially important. These events indicated that the Soviets had no interest in supporting Chinese expansion at the risk of clashing with the United States. They confirmed China's growing suspicion that the Kremlin put its relations with the United States, as they affected Russia's special national interests, ahead of the interests of the world communist movement. Not that China was any more eager than Russia to risk a nuclear war; rather, it was much more confident that the Soviet Union's professed nuclear superiority following Sputnik could support an active program of revolution and subversion by deterring American counterintervention.

The second Berlin crisis, which Khrushchev began in 1958, and the Cuban missile crisis, which he generated in 1962, indicated that the Soviet Union was not reluctant to play nuclear blackmail against the United States when its own interests were involved. Indeed, the Cuban crisis, arising primarily from Khrushchev's desire to enhance Russia's political leverage in Berlin and elsewhere by restoring its reputation for at least nuclear parity after the Kennedy administration's public disclosure of American superiority, displayed an adventurousness quite alien to China's calculating "realism."

In the aftermath of the Cuban fiasco, however, Soviet leaders seem to have decided that such confrontations were unprofitable and too risky. They switched to a strategy of détente with the West. In doing so, they further alienated China, which denounced Soviet policy as a conspiracy with the United States to put the interests of the superpowers above the interests of world revolution. With the atmospheric nuclear test ban and other steps toward a Soviet-American détente, the Sino-Soviet schism became increasingly public, acrimonious, and far-ranging. The two allies openly engaged in competition for the allegiance of, and control over, communist parties throughout the world, thereby creating Soviet-oriented, Chinese-oriented, and a growing number of "nonaligned" or primarily locally-oriented communist parties. In China's border war against

India in 1962, the Kremlin went so far as to furnish India with military equipment, paralleling American assistance. Thus the polemics of Soviet and Chinese charges and countercharges of incorrect strategy, hegemony seeking, and ideological heresy reveal a fundamental divergence of interests. The Soviet Union, as a global power, is primarily interested in holding its allies in Eastern Europe, undermining NATO, and extending its influence in the Third World with a minimum risk of a military encounter. Toward these ends it prefers traditional diplomatic maneuvering, military and economic assistance, tests of will and nerve short of war when military and political conditions are suitable, and association with, or penetration of, a variety of nationalist regimes that promise to reduce Western influence and enhance Soviet influence. China, on the other hand, is interested in getting rid of the American presence in the Asian-Pacific area, attaining national territorial goals in Asia, and becoming the world leader of the communist revolution in the Third World. Toward these ends it concentrates on subversion and attempts to incite and capitalize upon national liberation wars conducted by local communist parties, while it builds a nuclear force that may some day become the basis for a bolder confrontation with the United States and for a more active diplomatic strategy. The Sino-Soviet split, then, is far more serious and consequential than the loosening of allied ties in Europe.

The widening of the split does not, however, lead necessarily to the permanent realignment of the communist allies against one another, nor does it preclude parallel policies. It may have weakened China's power of expansion in the short run, but it has not made it seem anything but menacing to the security of Asia in the long run. At the same time, the Sino-Soviet split does create a kind of tripolarity in Asia, which greatly alters the premise of communist solidarity upon which the American containment and alliance policy in that area were originally based. Tripolarity sets the stage for new alignments and, in the long run perhaps, new alliances in Asia. In the short run, it creates new possibilities of parallel United States–U.S.S.R. alignments, as with India. It does not, however, portend the classic reversal of alliances. The Russian and Chinese responses to America's involvement in Vietnam suggest some of the potentialities and limits of the Sino-Soviet split. China has been determined that the North Vietnamese regime should continue to fight indefinitely until it eliminates the American presence; but China itself, through weakness and a realistic assessment of opportunities, seems intent upon staying out of the war unless the defense of its borders should seem to require intervention, and it provides relatively little material assistance to Hanoi while advising the local vanguard of the revolution that success must depend chiefly on self-help. The Soviet Union undoubtedly encourages China's cautious abstention and tries to keep Hanoi's conduct of the war within safe limits, although it is also interested in having the United States tied down and defeated without leaving China paramount in the area. In any event, in view of its competition for the control of communist parties, the Kremlin can scarcely afford *not* to help a national liberation war, in the face of Chinese allegations that Soviet leaders have abandoned the interests of world communism for the sake of Russian interests. For both purposes—embarrassing the United States and gaining leverage in Hanoi and the rest of the Third World at the expense of China—the Soviet Union provides limited but conspicuous military assistance to Hanoi.

The war in Vietnam has thus fostered parallel Sino-Soviet opposition to the United States for significantly divergent and even antagonistic goals, as well as similar ones. At some point of escalation American military action might consolidate the Sino-Soviet alliance temporarily. But, like American containment of China in crises short of war, resolute but carefully limited American opposition to North Vietnam evidently puts additional strains on the alliance. So far, these strains have not increased the prospect of the Soviet Union's alignment with the United States against China or Hanoi to bring about a settlement or de-escalation. Yet they may have enhanced the prospect of eventual Soviet alignment with India and Japan for limited purposes, whether with respect to the war in Vietnam or for broader objectives, since Moscow will almost surely be looking for indigenous counterpoises to China that can also provide it with diplomatic access in Asia.

9. United States Alliance Policy in the Third World

As a whole, the extension of American alliances beyond the Western Hemisphere has enhanced deterrence (although American intervention in the Korean War was a more convincing demonstration of America's willingness to use force against direct aggression at points of peripheral strategic interest than any alliance could be). In some cases America's alliances have also served as useful restraints on allies, helping to stabilize international politics by giving the United States access to, and influence upon, governments with potentially disruptive local grievances and ambitions. On the other hand, these alliances have not been free of difficulties and disadvantages. The liabilities of alliance have been most conspicuous in SEATO and CENTO.

In the non-European areas brought under the American deterrent umbrella at the height of the cold war, states lack a solid multilateral consensus of security interests coincident with American interests, and their foreign policies are preponderantly locally oriented, heterogeneous, and often subordinate to internal concerns. The capacity of many of the less-developed countries to maintain internal security and stability, let alone to project power beyond their borders, is tenuous or completely lacking. The practical and emotional reasons for nonalignment are still widely persuasive, even though the mystique has waned.

These characteristics of the Third World limit the capacity of the United States to organize effective counterpoises (if only as passive instruments for the projection of American power) against the Soviet Union or China by any means, but especially by alliances. They also mean that American alliances and efforts to form alliances tend to disturb local political patterns in ways that may be counterproductive. To make an alliance is to change the local balance of power and become involved in an ally's special concerns. The impact of an alliance on local configurations of power and interest may create new insecurities and aggravate old animosities in such a way as to antagonize disadvantaged states and even facilitate the penetration of a competing adversary. Thus the attempt of the United States to recruit Iraq in a multilateral Middle Eastern alliance alienated Egypt and facilitated the Soviet Union's active intervention in Middle Eastern politics by an arms assistance agreement with Egypt. The United States military assistance agreement and alliance with Pakistan alienated India. Conversely, when the United States extended military assistance to India in its border war with China, Pakistan began aligning itself with China and then Russia.

To be sure, America's participation in NATO also involves it in the relations of its allies with one another and sometimes, as in the case of the MLF's impact on Franco-German relations, accentuates tension between them. But in NATO the adverse effects of America's involvement are limited because interallied conflicts and rivalries do not entail threats to security or competitive arming and because they take place within an over-all consensus about the primacy of common security against the latent threat from a single adversary.

Thus, the critical difference between Europe and most of the rest of the world, so far as the feasibility and utility of alliances are concerned, can be expressed in terms of the structure of power and interests. In Europe the dominant pattern of international politics that springs from the major enmities and amities has been bipolar. The organization and management of military power and commitments has reflected this bipolarity. However, in most of the recently colonial areas outside Europe, the pattern of politics is fragmented and the distribution and control of military power are diffused among many states (insofar as one can properly speak of military power at such a low level of capability beyond state borders). The bipolar (or, with the Sino-Soviet split, increasingly tripolar) cold war contest, which is global, overlies this local pattern and interacts with it but does not absorb it or dominate it. Consequently, the United States has been confronted with the problem of meshing the two spheres of politics in such a way as to serve its primary objective of containing the expansion—by subversion, revolution, and war—of communist control. This is something of a problem even in NATO, since American involvements outside Europe reflect a global interest in containment that is not shared to the same extent by its allies. But the problem of meshing is much more troublesome outside Europe where American and local interests within an area frequently diverge. The problem is complicated by the fact that these states are of interest to the principals in the cold war not only as explicit or tacit collaborators against the adversary; their friendship and allegiance are also regarded as valuable stakes of politics in themselves. Hence, the United States has felt all the more need to defer to local interests and emotions in pursuing its global interests.

The United States made its first ambitious effort to mesh the local and global spheres of politics after the Korean War when the Eisenhower administration set out to recruit Asian and Middle Eastern participants in regional alliances that included Western powers. Dulles hoped that the alliances would become focuses of regional cohesion oriented in an anticommunist direction, and he frowned on nonalignment as an obstruction to this end. His effort at alliance-building failed to foster regional cohesion or to subordinate local divisions to global concerns, but it left the United States with points of contact and access that were useful in extending and reinforcing containment.

Under the Kennedy administration the United States, while holding on to viable allied contacts along the Asian periphery but refraining from any attempt to transform SEATO and CENTO into effective multilateral organizations, set out to mesh the local and global spheres of politics by a more determined effort to associate itself with the local interests of nonaligned states in economic development and national independence, hoping that this would create the most effective local resistance to communist penetration. To bolster the military component of containment, it relied chiefly on stabilizing the military balance with the Soviet Union on the basis of American nuclear superiority and building up mobile conventional and unconventional war forces to counter communist-supported local wars in the peripheral areas. Kennedy hoped that this strategy, coupled with the strategy of building local situations of economic strength, would enable the United States, in effect, to insulate large parts of the Third World from the cold war contest—at least so far as subversion and revolutionary war were concerned.

At present it appears that, so far as the American and Soviet contest is concerned, a kind of balance of power in the Third World has been achieved, although the Kremlin does not accept the balance as a basis for détente in the area. Consolidated by the Cuban missile crisis, the balance is marked by the failure of the Soviet Union to establish any outright communist state other than Cuba outside the postwar bloc occupied by the Red Army, and by mutually limited, though relentless, competition—largely by means of economic and military assistance, propaganda, and diplomacy—in the less-developed countries. It is also marked by Soviet caution in avoiding involvement in, or the escalation of, national liberation wars and local interstate wars.

Yet the militancy of China, its uncompromising commitment to leading the revolutionary expansion of the communist sphere of control in the less-developed areas, and its emergence as a strategic nuclear power, together with the repercussions of the expanded war in Vietnam, have called into question the adequacy of the Kennedy formula. If these developments pose a new threat of communist expansion—something that is unclear at this point—the United States, acting on the basis of its present broad policy objectives of preserving international order against expansion by communist states, would find itself the principal counterpoise to communist states in Asia but under conditions far less congenial to the effective use of American power than in Europe or, for that matter, in Korea and the Straits of Formosa. The question would then arise of whether another extension of American commitments were necessary and feasible and, if so, by what means. The answer to this question is complicated by the Sino-Soviet breach, the divergencies between other communist states and parties, the declining appeal of nonalignment, the possible development of more nearly autonomous intraregional balance-of-power systems, and the potential emergence of new centers of military (including nuclear) power and active political influence in Asia. It is further complicated by the fact that the war in Vietnam, whatever its course, seems destined to raise a question about American commitments in the context of an over-all reassessment of American interests and policies in the Third World. The nature and extent of American commitments in the future are therefore shrouded in the mystery of how national opinion will react to external conditions that are largely beyond American control. Yet, however the mystery may unfold, it seems fairly clear that the future of alliances in United States policy will not be a repetition of the past.

CHAPTER
VI

THE FUTURE OF ALLIANCES

1. *Possible Trends in the International Environment*

The history of alliances in the cold war indicates that the changing structure of power and pattern of conflict will have a decisive effect upon the nature and role of alliances in the future. Yet possible trends in the structure of power and the pattern of conflict are too numerous and varied to examine thoroughly in this study. I shall simply indicate, in cursory fashion, the variety of international environments that such trends *might* create within the next decade or two and suggest the most *likely* environment that is also compatible with American interests and within the capacity of the United States to promote.

But first, to provide some realistic limits to speculation, I shall assume the existence of several key features of the international environment during this period:

(1) The United States will remain a global power; that is, it will retain important interests in all parts of the world, and it will have the will and capacity to project its military and other instruments of power to all parts of the world where there is a reasonable chance that its power will support friendly states against coercion by states hostile to American aims and interests.

The steady economic and technological growth rate of the United States and the continued advance of the speed, range, and efficiency of weapons systems and of transportation and communication leave no doubt that the material basis of American global power will persist and grow. If the United States ceases to be a global power, it will be because of a deliberate retrenchment. Retrenchment might be encouraged by profound foreign frustrations and disappointments, by a radical decline of the communist threat and the absence of other threats of aggression and revolution by hostile states, by the emergence of new centers of power congenial to American interests that would fill in "power vacuums" in critical areas, or by any or all of these developments combined with America's preoccupation with a severe domestic crisis. Yet even in the face of these developments, the United States would probably continue to think of itself as a world power, no matter how much more selective it might become in exercising that power. The nation has ceased defining its security interests as purely continental or hemispheric for too long to revert to that minimal conception as long as it has the physical capacity to support a global role. American interests are now equivalent to the maintenance of an international order that is compatible with the support of American commitments, the prevention, limitation, or insulation of war, and the preservation of local balances of power against the threat of hegemony by any hostile regional power. American interests are comparable to those of imperial responsibility although they are nonimperialistic. Like literal imperial authority, responsibility of this sort is abdicated only in the face of the most severe economic, military, and political obstacles.

(2) The United States will continue to be the major noncommunist protagonist in an over-all conflict of virtually global scope; and for the next decade or more, whatever other conflicts may arise, this dominant conflict will be between the United States and friendly states, on the one hand, and the Soviet Union, China, and the smaller communist states, pursuing increasingly divergent policies, on the other hand.

The persistence of organized religious and ideological movements, even in the face of military defeats and schisms and despite the erosion and corruption of doctrine, is a familiar phenomenon in history. The communist movement—with its secular-scientific-missionary doctrine that promises deliverance from misery to most of the world's population, who live with unfulfilled and perhaps unfulfillable expectations of national autonomy and material progress—seems to be sufficiently responsive to modern aspirations, sufficiently adaptable to a variety of conditions, and sufficiently powerfully supported by the Soviet Union and China to be no exception to this phenomenon. This does not exclude the possibility, even likelihood, of the decline and disintegration of the communist movement as an expansionist force. It does not exclude limited American co-operation with the Soviet Union and other communist states, sometimes in alignment against another communist state. But it does indicate that during the next decade or two communist parties and states will remain the primary threat to American interests.

The very facts that the Soviet Union has the capacity to devastate the United States and that China will probably be able to inflict considerable nuclear damage on American cities before the end of the next decade, together with the fact that both states are determined to eliminate the power of the United States to affect affairs in what they conceive to be their special spheres of influence and security, seem sufficient to sustain the dominance of the cold war in one form or another for many years.

(3) Most of Asia, the Middle East, Africa, and Latin America will remain poor economically, weak militarily, and unstable politically. Although a very few presently underdeveloped states may achieve self-sustaining growth, the disparity between their standard of living and that of the advanced states will continue to increase. Consequently, few of the presently less-developed countries will have the prerequisites for participating with a significant military component in local balances of power based on a coherent pattern of align-

ments and alliances, and fewer still will be capable of affecting the global or regional balances of power, except indirectly through local conflicts that involve the superpowers and middle-range states.

(4) The superpowers and the major advanced states of Europe and the Asian-Pacific area (Japan, China, and Australia) will have the economic security and strength, military potential, political institutions, foreign policy elites, and experience with power politics to enable them to pursue well-articulated foreign policies supported by military power. But Western Europe will remain unique as a culturally and politically homogeneous region of advanced states capable of relating to each other closely, responsibly, and harmoniously on the diplomatic, economic, and military levels of policy, both bilaterally and in multilateral organizations. Like Asia increasingly, it will also be notable for the capacity of powerful states to engage in organized animosities that could quickly throw the whole world into political turmoil and general war.

If these are key factors affecting the future of alliances during the next decade or so, they still leave room for a wide variety of international environments. Merely adumbrating this variety may serve as an antidote to misplaced confidence in predictions about the complexities of international politics.

So far as the relations of the superpowers are concerned, one can reasonably imagine, for example: (1) *a tendency toward global tripolarity,* with China gaining primacy over the Soviet Union in Asia and the Third World and exerting such pressure against Soviet and American interests as to diminish their power substantially in other areas; (2) *a reversion to simple bipolarity,* caused either by *(a)* China's internal weakness, its loss of influence with neutralist and communist states and parties outside Asia, and increasing Soviet influence with noncommunist states and communist parties along the perimeter of China, or by *(b)* the restoration of Sino-Soviet collaboration; (3) *the decline of both Russia and China to essentially regional powers* with waning control over increasingly differentiated and nationalistic communist parties beyond the reach of their direct military support, leaving the United States the globally preponderant military power; (4) *the extension of the Soviet-American détente leading to a kind of duopoly* in world politics, based on diplomatic collaboration in containing China, tacit agreement upon spheres of regional primacy, reciprocally limited intervention in the Third World, and co-operation in isolating and pacifying the crises and wars of other states; or (5) *the retrenchment of both the United States and the Soviet Union from intervention in the Third World,* except by economic and diplomatic means, because of widespread chaos and a lack of sufficient political dividends to warrant the risks of military involvement.

Interacting with the relations of the superpowers, many possible trends in the structure of power and patterns of conflict among the major states of Europe might develop; for example: (1) *a tendency toward de facto nonalignment or political realignment and decentralization in NATO and the WTO,* leaving the United States and the Soviet Union with preponderance in maintaining the military balance but with decreasing influence over the military and diplomatic policies of the states in their respective spheres of interest; (2) *the severe fragmentation of Eastern Europe by national political and territorial conflicts,* leading to either the reassertion of Soviet physical control or the elimination of Soviet authority; (3) *the creation of a Western European union, federation, or confederation,* which would gradually displace the United States as the preponderant noncommunist military power in Europe; (4) *a European settlement based on the reunification of Germany* and accompanied by the subordination of the cold war to regional issues, especially the issue of Germany's position in Europe; (5) *a crisis created by Germany's turn toward the Soviet Union* for satisfaction of basic national goals.

Similarly, in Asia, the Middle East, Africa, and Latin America a number of different developments might shape the international environment; for example: (1) *accentuated subnational (personal, tribal, religious, and ethnic) and transnational (including antiwhite) conflicts,* marked by many coups and subversions, and possibly general chaos, but not by further development of well-defined national conflicts or coherent local balances of power between governments that clearly represent state interests; (2) *the emergence of more clearly defined territorial conflicts* and a few locally dominant states with the capacity to project power beyond their borders, which would lead to the crystallization of local and regional patterns of power politics, including the development of rudimentary balance of power systems; (3) *the formation of cohesive multilateral regional organizations* capable of fostering international order among their members, limiting extraregional intervention, and enhancing their bargaining power with advanced states outside the region; and (4) *the emergence of Japan, Australia, and possibly India as major participants in a multipolar Asian balance of power,* along with China, Russia, and the United States.

Different combinations and interactions of these three sets of environmental possibilities and their many variants could produce a great variety of political and military conditions affecting American commitments. One can imagine world politics revolving around intense superpower competition or United States–Chinese competition in the Third World; the problems of constructing order and making American preponderance acceptable in a world dominated by pervasive American influence; an American-Soviet entente engaged in preventing the endemic disorders of the less-developed world from spilling over into the developed areas; a tripolar or multipolar struggle for power in Asia, the Middle East, and Africa; great-power realignment in Europe and Asia; or the emergence of the once-great states of Europe as major actors in Africa and of Japan in Southeast Asia and the Pacific. But the multiplicity of alternative environments is impossibly unwieldy to examine in a general essay. Therefore, as a working hypothesis, I shall briefly describe the structure of power and the pattern of conflict that seem most likely to develop in the next ten or fifteen years, yet that—to make allowance for both preferences and realism—are also compatible with basic American interests and within the capacity of the United States to promote.

2. The Likely International Environment

For the next decade, at least, the United States will retain an over-all global superiority to the Soviet Union and China —a superiority marked by America's immense, unrivaled economic and technological strength and by its unequaled capacity to utilize this strength and project it overseas in the form of economic and military power. The very possession of this power, even though its effective use may be increasingly constrained by intractable local conflicts and the self-assertiveness of small states, will sustain America's vital interest in a minimal degree of international order throughout the world.

One can expect Soviet leaders to try to offset this primacy by seeking dramatic gains in military technology, inciting crises to test American resolution, playing upon divergencies in Western Europe (especially by manipulating the German lever), and intervening in the Third World with military assistance and, as overseas capabilities grow, with supplies, weapons, technicians, and even troops, in order to exploit nationalist revolutions and conflicts among small states. Soviet exploitation of these options seems likely to make an increasing amount of trouble for the United States. Yet the Soviet Union will not be able to challenge American paramountcy seriously or to overcome the many obstacles to the expansion of the limited area of Soviet primacy. Not the least of these obstacles will be the continued necessity, from Moscow's standpoint, of perpetuating an over-all strategy of détente, if only because of the risks of war with the United States, the dangers of overinvolvement in unmanageable local conflicts, and Soviet preoccupation with China and Eastern Europe.

The Soviet Union will enjoy primacy in its struggle with China for control of communist parties in the less-developed areas outside Asia—and perhaps in Asia as well—depending in part on the flexibility of Chinese leadership and the outcome of the Vietnam war. It will also be a major diplomatic influence in the Middle East and Asia. But it will not succeed in establishing controllable dependencies in the Third World as the independence of local revolutionary movements and national communist states from Soviet influence continues to grow, providing the United States displays the proper combination of resolve, caution, and selectivity in undertaking political and military counterintervention.

The United States will retain paramountcy in Latin America, but its power will be circumscribed by local nationalism and by great restraints upon direct or indirect military intervention. Latin America will probably experience considerable economic and social unrest; but, despite subversive efforts by communist and other leftist parties, the area will remain largely outside the mainstream of international politics. Although national rivalries and political alignments in Latin America may grow sharper, they will not lead to anything approaching a subsystem of power politics with competitive arming and indigenous alliances.

Whereas the United States will enjoy relatively secure primacy in its metaphorical backyard in the Western Hemisphere, the Soviet Union will face distracting problems in both its backyard (Asia) and its frontyard (Eastern Europe). In its frontyard the Soviet problem will be to retain the allegiance, co-operation, and cohesion of allies without reverting to brute force; but in its backyard it will have to contend with China, which will continue to view its relations with the Soviet Union as a struggle for hegemony in the communist system, particularly in Asia.

China, despite its size, the determination of its leadership, the discipline of its population, and its ability to concentrate resources for military purposes, will not approach the economic or military strength of Russia or the potential of Japan in the next decade. Nevertheless, it will be a formidable and growing threat to the security of all states on or near its perimeter, including the Soviet Union, as it strives to eliminate or neutralize the influence of all major states in Asia, bring Taiwan within its orbit, sustain and advance revolutionary activity abroad, and establish its paramountcy in Asia. It will be a threat, whether or not a more moderate regime comes into power. Indeed, united under any strong nationalist regime, China would in some measure challenge the security of its Asian neighbors.

For a decade China may not have the strength or inclination to use its own armed forces directly to change the status quo, at least not beyond the scale of its incursions along the Indian and Burmese borders. Among the existing and potential proxies for China, North Vietnam is unique in that it is an effective nationalist regime with a first-rate army. Yet, because of the relative weakness of the states near China's border and China's development of a nuclear force that by the 1970's will be able to threaten considerable devastation in the Asian-Pacific area and impose additional caution on the United States, China is bound to create a sense of insecurity throughout the region. This insecurity can only be allayed by the existence of convincing military counterpoises. As China's long-range nuclear capability increases, it will call into serious question the credibility and relevance of America's nuclear forces as a counterpoise to conventional and unconventional incursions supported by China.

By the end of the 1980's China might become sufficiently powerful—internally, regionally, and in long-range striking power—to be a factor in the global balance, rivaling the Soviet Union. In that case, the United States, the Soviet Union, and China would be engaged in a tripolar pattern of shifting conflicts and alignments in which each would try to prevent the other two from aligning against it, yet each would seek the alignment of another. This pattern, possibly modified by the active participation of Japan in the Asian balance of power, would then be the primary reference point for the politics of regional and local powers. In this multipolar context China might be induced or compelled to abandon its revolutionary and hegemonial ambitions in favor of orthodox *Realpolitik*.

In the next decade of general unrest and disorder in Asia the Soviet Union will probably wish to discourage or contain local revolutions and wars that risk the direct involvement of Chinese or Soviet forces, but it will also be interested in encouraging such disturbances to the extent that they tie down American power and embarrass the United States politically without incurring excessive risks of a direct Soviet-United States confrontation. Therefore Soviet concern over Chinese ambitions and adventures will not completely overcome Soviet-American competition in Asia; nor will it induce a Soviet withdrawal from Eastern Europe or a realignment with the United States. Rather, Sino-Soviet tension will reinforce the Soviet desire to hold on to Eastern Europe and to demonstrate that bloc members can satisfy their national interests within the Soviet commonwealth.

In Europe the United States and the Soviet Union will continue to be the mainstays of a stable military balance within the existing alliance structure. As military organizations, NATO and WTO will in some diminished form institutionalize the military predominance of the superpowers and provide a multilateral framework for continued bilateral American-FRG collaboration and the parallel Soviet-GDR tie. United States and Soviet forces, possibly in reduced numbers, will remain in the two Germanies as assurance of the military paramountcy of the superpowers

and their continuing restraint of the two Germanies.
Both alliances will break down into a set of more clearly
differentiated bilateral relations. Key allies will become
more independent and active politically, as East-West and
interallied relations become the chief political concerns.
Political polycentrism and realignment will take place
despite military bipolarity. Some allies—most probably
France and Rumania, one would judge from present trends
—might become, in effect, nonaligned states under superpower protection.

One might describe the resulting structure of power in
Europe as consisting of politically more decentralized and
differentiated alignments within a bipolar military balance
organized in two residual multilateral alliances led by two
militarily dominant powers. Despite the political ferment
generated by this more pluralistic configuration, increased
diplomatic activity is not likely to produce formal political
changes. Thus no formal settlement of the division of Germany seems likely. Yet the two Germanies will come into
closer touch with each other, both as governments and as
nations, while remaining sovereign states. Whether this leads
to new tensions or a rapprochement between them, the
growing weight of the two Germanies in the center of the
delicately balanced European scales is destined to be the
focal point of European power politics in the relatively fluid
and unstructured environment of the next decade or so.

In the very long run—say, twenty or twenty-five years—a
Western European coalition capable of providing its own
conventional and nuclear protection, with only marginal dependence on the United States, might emerge. There are a
number of factors that favor such a development: combined
resources, political capacity, alliance-mindedness, cultural
affinity, sense of Europeanism, and progress toward economic
integration in Western Europe. Nevertheless, there are
probably insuperable obstacles to the creation of a Western
European military union: (1) Historically, federation or
confederation of states has taken place only under very spe-

cial conditions, most of which do not exist in Western Europe. (2) On the level of high politics and defense, national differences and the tendency to assert them are becoming more marked among the major Western European states. (3) In a period of détente there is insufficient incentive to form a new military union, and there are many domestic and foreign reasons not to form one. (4) A military union would have to establish a common nuclear force, but overwhelming difficulties impede any group of states—especially states that think of themselves as roughly equal—from sharing satisfactorily decisions governing the use of nuclear weapons; for none would agree to a nuclear war against its will, yet none would agree to let another state veto its use of nuclear weapons.

Whatever happens in Europe, the United States, as a global power, will be as intensely concerned with the Third World as ever. But its policies in the Third World will become increasingly differentiated as the things that distinguish various regions and countries become increasingly more significant than the things they have in common.

Relations among states in the Middle East will continue to revolve around Arab-Israeli hostility and an uneasy, shifting balance of political rivalries, accompanied by competitive arming. No state will emerge as dominant, and no military coalitions or political unification movements will emerge to consolidate alignments. In this fragmented and competitive environment the Soviet Union, lacking other promising opportunities for expanding its domain, may for historic and geopolitical reasons focus its chief effort to project power beyond the heartland of Eurasia upon the Middle East by manipulating military assistance and maneuvering diplomatically among local conflicts and alignments against the background of an impressive Soviet naval presence in the Mediterranean.

The Arab-Israeli conflict will not abate. The prospect of its erupting in renewed warfare will increase if Israel's production of nuclear weapons becomes imminent. But a combination of Israel's military strength, the American-Soviet military-assistance balance, and the superpowers' diplomatic intervention may succeed in preserving an uneasy peace in which the implicit threat of nuclear armament will play a restraining role.

Under these conditions the United States will be drawn, perforce, into more active intervention by one means or another in the internal and international politics of the area. Thus the United States and the Soviet Union will be major competitors in an international subsystem that will be neither independent of, nor determined by, the global sphere of politics. For this reason the Middle East will present the greatest danger of an American-Soviet crisis or war growing out of commitments to local states over which neither state has much control.

The new states of Africa will remain too weak, disorganized, and remote from the centers of world power, and their political relations will be too erratic, to provide incentives equal to those in the Middle East for intervention by extraregional states. The interstate politics of Africa will be heavily infused with tribal and factional conflict. Local politics will intersect world politics on the plane of colonial, neocolonial, and racial issues, but none of these issues will provide the basis for the kinds of coalitions or pan-African organizations that could effectively concert military power or diplomacy. Instead, a host of local national and subnational issues, ranging from border conflicts to federation and defederation, will render the particular issues of unity, development, and security more concrete and pressing than the general issues of North-South, rich-poor relations.

In the long run, in two or three decades, this political introversion might lead to loose regional and subregional groupings, which would provide the framework within which more coherent patterns of international politics and semiautonomous balance-of-power systems could emerge. If a few states, such as Algeria, Nigeria (despite its present disintegration), Kenya, and Tanzania, were cohesive nations with stable and efficient governments, they might act as political centers to speed the formation of international subsystems comparable to the one that may develop in the Middle East. However, the process of international-system-building, like the process of state- and nation-building upon which it depends, is almost sure to be marked by considerable violence. This violence will engage the interests and attention of the United States, the Soviet Union, and China. If any of these states should adopt a policy of active military intervention by direct or indirect means, for whatever reason, it might touch off a postcolonial contest that would have serious repercussions upon the global balance of power. But such a development seems unlikely, if only because the inchoate and volatile nature of African politics, both internal and external, renders such intervention an unreliable instrument of policy.

In Africa and in other parts of the former colonial world, the once-great European states might promote a more stable and structured pattern of alignments if they were to become more active participants in local and regional politics, exerting their economic and military power by means of a variety of arrangements, short of formal alliance, with indigenous states and regimes. On the other hand, they might also only aggravate the fragmentation of politics if the local states and regimes were not strong enough to enter into fairly equal relationships with the donors on the basis of coherent national policies. But if the present steady withdrawal of most of the middle-range states, like France and England, from active participation in the politics of Asia, the Middle East, and Africa could be reversed so that these states became major but not dominant weights in indigenous balances of power, the United States might be spared some of the hazards and burdens that accompany its present position as the preponderant Western extraregional power in these unsettled areas and virtually the only military counterpoise to the Soviet Union and China. This presumes, of course, not only that the middle-range states would be willing and able to take on some of these hazards and burdens, largely for the sake of enhancing their status, but also that the superpowers would be willing to let these states become major actors in spheres of current competition. Present tendencies do not support either of these suppositions.

Only in Asia is there much prospect in the next decade of the development of a full-fledged multipolar pattern of international politics, in the sense of several states exercising advanced military power in pursuit of independent interests within a pattern of political interaction in which none is clearly dominant. The principal poles of power in this hypothetical environment would be the United States, China, the Soviet Union, and a rearmed and politically active Japan, with Australia and possibly India (if it enjoys internal cohesion, vigorous national leadership, and a growing economy) playing secondary roles. Perhaps some loose quasi-military subregional groupings would also exert some political weight. Fear of China would be the initial catalyst for such a multipolar pattern of politics, but the interests of the other powers would be sufficiently differentiated to complicate the common opposition to Chinese hegemony with other conflicts and alignments.

Yet present realities raise doubts that the potential threat of China in Asia will soon arouse the kind of concern for military security in Japan, India, or other Asian states that could overcome all the psychological and political obstacles to their playing an active balance-of-power role. For the next decade the main actors defining the pattern of conflict and the structure of power in Asia will probably be only the United States, the Soviet Union, and China, with Japan and India playing much more limited political roles similar to those of the principal states in Europe, so that there will be a politically qualified military tripolarity in Asia corresponding to the qualified bipolarity in Europe.

This sketch of a likely pattern of power politics in the future suggests a continuation of the American-Soviet contest on the basis of a fairly stable military-political equilib-

rium and limited co-operation far short of a global duopoly
or entente. It supposes that the United States will be superior to the Soviet Union in its capacity to project power to
remote parts of the world but that Russia will nevertheless
be the major rival of the United States, and occasionally its
chief accomplice, in most parts of the world. However,
China, which has already replaced Russia as the active ideological and revolutionary power, may become one of the
three major transregional as well as regional powers in the
next two decades.

Asia will become the center of the cold war within an
increasingly complex and fluid configuration of power and
interests. European politics will revolve around the diplomatic and intra-alliance problems of consolidating a détente
and seeking new political alignments within the bipolar
structure of military power. Most of the Third World will
be preoccupied with local and domestic issues in which the
competition between the United States, the Soviet Union
and China will intrude but not to the extent of dominating
the shifting conflicts and alignments.

If a pattern of international politics like this develops, it
will further complicate and diversify the objectives and
strategies of American policy as compared to those of the
earlier phases of the cold war when the dominant problem
was to build deterrents against the Soviet Union and then
against China, and when China seemed to be the subordinate partner in a communist bloc that was united except
for Yugoslavia. As a result, Soviet-American relations will
tend to become a more complex blend of competition and co-
operation, less ideologically oriented and more like nine-
teenth-century *Realpolitik*. Communist efforts to exploit
anti-Western nationalism and aspirations for modernization
in the Third World will continue. But the Sino-Soviet competition, the growing divergencies among communist parties, the emergence of more self-reliant reform and revolutionary movements rooted in local conditions, and the loss of

confidence and repute which any messianic movement that fails to deliver the promised land must eventually suffer, may gradually sap the vitality of communist revolutionary parties while impeding either the Soviet Union or China from extending their spheres of control and influence beyond a few adjacent areas by subversion, political penetration, or national wars of liberation.

The limitations upon the power of communist states and parties in the Third World reflect the fact that among the poor, weak, new states, as among the advanced states, the pattern of international politics is growing more complicated and, in a way, more traditional in terms of historic experience than the pattern that seemed to be emerging after the Korean War. In other words, world politics will probably not be oriented chiefly about a North-South, rich-poor, colonial-anticolonial, white-colored, or revolutionary-nonrevolutionary axis. Nor will the Third World be the decisive arena of a bipolar or even tripolar extension of the cold war. Rather, the economic, political, and racial issues implicit in this image of polarized politics will be overlaid by, and suffused with, various issues of national security, status, and nation-building. Regimes that hope to be reasonably successful will have to face their internal problems with less dependence on panaceas or radical ideologies, less addiction to the personal trappings of charismatic leadership, and more attention to the prosaic business of efficient government. Yet one cannot now be confident that many, or indeed any, will follow this prescription. One can only expect that the old prescriptions of an earlier phase in the cold war will become obsolete.

This reorientation of foreign policies and expectations in the Third World will render the distinctive political characteristics of various regions, subregions, and states more and more conspicuous as compared to their common sentiments and visions. Hopefully, it might enable their relations with the advanced states to proceed on a more pragmatic and less emotional basis. One aspect of this pragmatism could be a tendency to reinvolve former metropoles and other great powers in local and regional politics on a practical *quid pro quo* basis. Whether or not such a reorientation led to coherent subsystems of international politics, American-Soviet competition in the area would probably be limited and fairly stable rather than intense and adventurous.

The most consequential changes in the pattern of power and conflict in the Third World will take place along the peripheries of China. But there the local issues will be absorbed in emerging multipolar conflicts and alignments in which the traditional issues of power, security, and status among advanced states will predominate. In many ways the international politics of the Third World, like the politics of the advanced states, will bear more resemblance to patterns of the eighteenth or nineteenth centuries than to that of the familiar cold war. But the safest prediction to make is that twenty years from now some quite new pattern, perhaps one as different from any previous period of modern history as the present is from the beginning of the cold war, will have begun to emerge.

One of the factors that have accelerated change and complicated predictions in international politics in modern times is the rapid development of military technology. Many assumptions about technological factors are implicit in the preceding survey. One assumption is that advances in offensive and defensive strategic nuclear capabilities—for example, in multiple warheads (MIRV), ballistic missile defense (BMD), space reconnaissance, and lasers—will not upset the American-Soviet balance in the sense that either state will be more willing, or will think that the other is more willing, to initiate the use of nuclear weapons under any circumstances. Another assumption is that these advances will not make alliances obsolete by rendering the protection of other states by superpowers ineffectual or giving other states equality with the superpowers or autonomy in security. Related to this proposition is the supposition that new and improved weapons will not in general narrow the disparities of effective power between superpowers, second-rank once-great states, and less-developed countries—although Japan and conceivably China might join the ranks of the superpowers in the next twenty-five years.

I shall not examine these assumptions. The assessment of technological developments and their effects upon the structure of power and international politics is a very large subject in itself. But three technological developments are of sufficient importance to the future of alliances to single out for brief discussion—overseas transport capabilities, the prospect of nuclear proliferation, and improved defenses against long-range missiles.

3. Overseas Transport Capabilities

Advancements in aerotransport capabilities will have a significant military payoff for the United States in that they will permit it to deploy quickly, from its interior zone to distant points, forces capable of demonstrating military resolve, conveying deterrence, relieving local forces for combat, responding rapidly to crises, executing holding actions, and sustaining local military operations. Advanced airlift technology—in conjunction with sealift capabilities, the development of floating bases to support aircraft, missiles, and marine forces, and further pre-positioning of logistic stockpiles in dispersed and protected areas—could relieve the United States of military dependence upon many of its remaining overseas air and ground-force bases. It will add an important new dimension of flexibility that is required to support many different kinds of military tasks in remote places at all levels of conflict and in varied physical and political conditions. Cost factors require this process to take place over a number of years, but the economic and technological capacity to put it into effect exists. Indeed, the process has already begun.[1] The airlift capability of the future will be expanded by a number of developments. Much heavier weights will be carried farther and faster in large transports when the gigantic C-5A joins the C-141 in 1968.[2] Development of supersonic transports in the 1970's would improve airlift performance further. In the more distant future, dramatic developments such as an intercontinental aerospacecraft (ICARUS) are anticipated. Vertical take-off and landing (VTOL) features will be incorporated into increasingly larger aircraft that will have greater weight-carrying capabilities over long distances. Under development are command and control centers and links that can be transported by air or aerospace and will reduce the need for overland communication links and for military command headquarters and subordinate control centers in the zone of engagement. Methods of detailed reconnaissance from high aerospace will greatly reduce dependence upon ground-based radar and surveillance from the ground or low-flying aircraft.

Development of large sea barges and submarines may greatly enhance the capacity of the United States to transport men, supplies, and equipment. Thus the Department of Defense has sought appropriations for swift barge carriers (called FDL's, for fast deployment logistics ships), which could carry critical supplies and station them in forward areas. For at least a decade, sea transport will be more economical than airlift for many purposes, and it may always be

1. According to *Aviation Daily,* December 20, 1966, United States military airlift capability increased 400 per cent in the four or five preceding years and would probably double in the next four years.

2. It is estimated that a build-up of overseas forces that would take more than a month with current sea- and airlift could be achieved in a week with 100 C-5As. Fewer than 100 C-5As could achieve the 1963 Operation Big Lift to Europe, which took 63 hours, in 24 hours. J. S. Butz, Jr., *Air Force/Space Digest International,* March, 1966.

so for bulk items like fuel and for the delivery of large quantities of men and goods over a period of a month or more. Moreover, it is not likely to suffer from restrictions comparable to those that are being increasingly imposed on airplanes by various countries that deny rights of overflight.

Improvements in air- and sealift mean that the value of an alliance or a particular ally to the United States, insofar as it is derived from the function of providing reconnaissance bases or horizontal access to a zone of potential military engagement, will be reduced. Consequently, the United States could introduce a militarily effective denial capability into a foreign area without pre-existing facilities or installations in that area, and a foreign nation could avail itself of this capability through an alliance with the United States without thereby incurring physical impingements on its territory. To the extent that allies or potential allies regard an American presence on their soil during peacetime as a political cost, trends in aerotransport technology can reduce that liability. They may also reduce the need for alliances or military assistance agreements when such arrangements would otherwise be necessary to acquire land or sea access.

Air- and sealift technology will also reduce the need for elaborate, relatively permanent, NATO-type physical infrastructures. It will enable planning and co-ordination to be carried out primarily on paper, supplemented by occasional joint maneuvers. The visible physical apparatus of alliances or military assistance agreements—bases, supply lines, and so forth—can then be substantially diminished. In particular, this trend applies to NATO, where the obsolescence of its elaborate infrastructure is being hastened by the virtual abandonment of the effort to establish a conventional force in Europe that is capable of fighting a limited war of any duration.

The declining utility of infrastructure will tend to reduce the costs of realignment and opting in or out of alliances. It will improve America's bargaining position with allies when adjusting terms of collaboration. It will mean that when there are political reasons for avoiding the tangible signs of interdependence the negotiation of alliance arrangements will not need to involve publics and parliaments as much as in the past. At the same time, advanced aerospace capabilities will increase the physical capacity of the United States to extend effective guarantees to distant states.

On the other hand, since technological military considerations are by no means the only ones affecting alliances, one must qualify all these possible implications of aerotransport and sealift advancements. Thus the stability or, from another perspective, inertia and inflexibility of alliances among advanced states depend upon some important factors other than the maintenance of infrastructures. Above all, they depend on the defensive and deterrent nature of alliances, for defensive alignments are apt to change less frequently than offensive alignments (especially those formed in preparation for a specific military action), and the need to sustain the credibility of deterrent commitments adds an incentive to prolong alliances and, in some cases, to use a visible means of implementing pledges to allies. Insofar as popular involvement has reduced the flexibility of alliances, it should be noted that, regardless of visible infrastructure or allied presence, national publics and parliaments are likely to become more rather than less involved in alliances, since the spread of popular government seems assured. Moreover, aside from the demands of horizontal access, the imperatives of dependable peacetime planning and co-ordination of armed forces, if only on paper, militate against the flexible opting in and out of alliances. Besides this factor, in the case of NATO the institutions as much as the infrastructure enhance its stability and endurance.

Furthermore, the history of NATO indicates that there are important reasons for maintaining armed forces overseas in addition to the facilitation of horizontal access to a zone of potential military engagement. One important purpose is to enhance deterrence by making the involvement of American forces in defense of allies more credible. Indeed, the very fact that the United States is obviously becoming less dependent on foreign bases and forces-in-being in order to meet overseas aggression, together with the fact that technology has long since largely relieved it from dependence on overseas bases and forces for protection of its own territory, reinforces allied apprehension and suspicion that the United States may not respond adequately (or may not convince adversaries that it will respond) to overseas aggression, especially to limited or ambiguous aggression.

American demonstrations of intent, peacetime maneuvers, and conspicuous preparations for airlift may not adequately compensate for the psychological disadvantage, in terms of possible provocation as well as loss of credibility, of having to move forces to a point of danger rather than having American forces already in the area. America's allies recognize that it may require an agonizing decision for the President of the United States to move forces to the scene of a crisis. They cannot count on forces stationed in the United States being earmarked for assistance to them in a time of competing needs. The importance of American forces in Europe is not primarily their speed of reaction to aggression but rather the assurance of their virtually automatic involvement in the event of aggression and their ability to test the potential aggressor's intentions by their very presence without generating the excitement and provocation of a major military maneuver.

Yet there are few places outside, and, indeed, not all places inside, the NATO area where the stationing of American forces is politically acceptable, and there are few places where potential military aggression would take a form that would require the almost automatic response that has seemed necessary in Europe. In any case, United States forces could not be stationed everywhere they might conceivably be needed. Moreover, outside Europe the need for

land access was never a decisive motive for alliances. For
local defense, primary reliance was put on local forces, supplemented by American air and sea power offshore and in
the continental United States. To some extent the extension
of American alliances to Asia was due to the need for bases,
but primarily it was an effort to enhance, by formal commitments, the credibility of America's determination to respond
to aggression.

Militarily, the Vietnam war and the situation immediately
following it will require American land bases and forces in
Asia—for example, in Thailand. In peacetime, however,
when the immediate military threat has subsided, they might
be a net political liability rather than a crucial asset as in
Europe. Where such a military presence would be a liability,
future aerotransport capabilities should enhance the capacity
of the United States to undertake politically useful military
commitments on a flexible basis in the Third World. Nevertheless, the United States will continue to need large bases
overseas, and in some cases, as in the Pacific area, formal
arrangements amounting to alliances will be politically useful in order to retain access to them. New aerotransport and
sealift capabilities will merely enable the United States to be
more selective in establishing and maintaining such bases
and commitments.

As the technology of overseas transportation will enhance
America's capacity to project its military power quickly,
under various circumstances, and for a variety of limited
objectives in the Third World, so it will also enhance the
Soviet capacity, which until now has been strikingly defi-
cient by comparison. In the next decade the Soviet Union
will not have the economic resources to undertake an airlift
and sealift program even approaching the dimensions of the
existing American program and still continue its vast expenditures on strategic weapons systems. But merely by continuing more modest improvements already in force and
recently begun—notably, in the merchant marine, amphibi-

ous craft, aircraft carriers, and super-airtransport—it can significantly increase its options to intervene in local crises, wars, and political windfalls. These increased options, coupled with the prospect of many local conflicts in Africa and elsewhere in which states and factions may seek Soviet assistance, will increase the risk of a direct or indirect American-Soviet local confrontation and complicate both the military and political environment of American policy in the Third World.

The chief effect of this development upon American commitments will probably be to enhance the utility of *ad hoc* political arrangements that are much less formal, permanent, and binding than alliances. Increased pressure for assistance upon both superpowers by local regimes promises to reinforce their desire to maintain the option of giving assistance while keeping their involvement as limited and flexible as possible.

4. *The Prospect of Nuclear Proliferation*

Like the effects of overseas transport capabilities on alliances, the likelihood that additional states will acquire nuclear weapons and the probable consequences of their doing so present problems of analysis far beyond technological prediction or strictly military considerations. Thus it is clear that the net political incentive or disincentive for a state to build nuclear weapons has been as important in determining the number of nuclear powers as the technological and economic capacity of states, since several non-nuclear states— Canada, West Germany, Japan, Italy, India, and Sweden—have at least as great a capability to acquire nuclear weapons as China.

In the next ten to fifteen years the spread of plutonium production for civilian energy will probably enable at least a dozen more states to build nuclear weapons with limited delivery capabilities if they should decide to make the effort. If all these states should rush into nuclear production as fast as they can, the impact upon international politics would surely be radical and perhaps violent. But it is more likely that the distribution and pace of nuclear acquisition will continue to be sufficiently limited and moderate to permit politics to adjust to nuclear proliferation without major upheavals. Among potential nuclear powers in the near future, only India, Japan, and Israel seem likely to have sufficient incentives to produce nuclear weapons, and each of these countries faces strong political disincentives. In any event, the balance of incentives and disincentives, unlike that in France, Britain, and China, will be complex and delicate.

Instinctively, the United States and the Soviet Union oppose the spread of nuclear weapons, not only because they do not want competition, but also because they have become very sensitive to the dangers of nuclear war and do not want the problem of keeping these dangers under control complicated by the addition of other fingers on nuclear triggers. When faced with specific nuclear candidates in specific political situations, however, their general opposition to additional nuclear forces may be overruled by calculations of the relative advantages and disadvantages of discouraging nuclear acquisition, passively accepting it, or even assisting it.

In trying to discourage nuclear candidates directly, the superpowers are in a poor political position because their efforts must bear the stigma of trying to perpetuate their duopoly at the expense of other states—a point that both allies and nonaligned have emphasized. In the case of some allies with the capacity to build nuclear weapons, who feel secure under a superpower's protection, who are absolutely dependent on its military and diplomatic support, and who have no strong incentives of status or prestige to become nuclear powers, the superpower may be able to counteract nuclear incentives by a combination of threats to restrict support if the state "goes nuclear" and promises to extend nuclear "sharing" and other rewards if it refrains. But the Soviet or American ability to discourage other nuclear aspirants from acquiring nuclear weapons is bound to be quite limited, whether they rely on nonproliferation agreements or informal pressures and inducements.

The inadequacy of nonproliferation treaties as disincentives to nuclear aspirants is suggested not only by the fact that France and China reject such treaties as discriminatory, but also by the fact that various non-nuclear nations in the Eighteen-Nation Disarmament Committee have insisted that their acceptance of nuclear prohibitions be linked with far-reaching constraints upon the nuclear powers, such as nuclear-free zones, a cutoff in the production of fissionable material, and a freeze on nuclear delivery vehicles. India, which is presently the country considering nuclear acquisition most actively, has suggested various compensations for a pledge of nuclear abstinence, including multilateral guarantees through the United Nations to protect non-nuclear against nuclear states.

Securing genuinely multilateral guarantees to non-nuclear states through the United Nations would be fruitless for the same reason that the Security Council cannot be expected to apply conventional force against a major aggressor: Among the major international competitors there are no common interests requiring the use of force that can be relied upon to take precedence over special national interests. On the other hand, guarantees by one, or possibly two, nuclear states might be a more efficacious compensation for nuclear abstinence. With this in mind, President Johnson in effect extended a unilateral guarantee to nuclear abstainers (directed especially, although not explicitly, at India) when, following the first Chinese atomic explosion, he announced in a national address on October 18, 1964, "The nations that do not seek national nuclear weapons can be sure that if they need our strong support against some threat of nuclear blackmail, then they will have it."

Yet there are important limitations on such unilateral or bilateral guarantees, whether formalized or not: (1) A guarantee would be addressed only to the security incentive for acquiring nuclear weapons, not to other motives such as status and independent political power. (2) A guarantee would be of questionable value for a nuclear aspirant's security because of the difficulty of making any promise to use nuclear weapons in behalf of another state credible and because of the virtually prohibitive difficulty of establishing credibility when a nuclear aspirant outside a zone of primary national interest to the nuclear power wants protection in the form of a first-strike deterrent to conventional aggression. (This kind of protection might interest India, for example, more than protection against a Chinese nuclear threat.) (3) Few nuclear aspirants that are not already allied will want to accept a formal nuclear guarantee from only the United States or the Soviet Union for fear of antagonizing one side or the other and becoming too closely involved in their conflicts; yet the credibility of a joint United States–Soviet Union guarantee would be highly questionable. (On the other hand, parallel guarantees by the United States and the Soviet Union may be acceptable to some nuclear abstainers, possibly including India.) (4) The superpowers will be reluctant to commit themselves in a formal agreement to use nuclear weapons in behalf of states with which they would not otherwise have a sufficient correspondence of vital interests to choose as allies. (5) Countervailing guarantees by the United States and the Soviet Union to competing protégés might involve the superpowers too deeply in minor power politics and could even lead to a direct confrontation, which a more detached position might avoid. (6) In extending commitments to a state that deliberately refrains from building nuclear weapons in return for a guarantee, nuclear powers would become vulnerable to awkward demands for material and political support as the price for continued abstinence.

Therefore, whether or not nuclear powers find guarantees wise in particular cases, guarantees are not likely to serve as general alternatives to nuclear proliferation because of the variety of political circumstances that govern the relations between potential guarantors and nuclear candidates. Correspondingly, when nuclear powers have to contemplate concrete courses of action with respect to potential nuclear powers, they will be governed by a variety of political considerations peculiar to each case, not merely by a general opposition to additional nuclear forces. In some cases the United States may extend loosely formulated unilateral guarantees of nuclear protection. In others it may threaten to apply political and economic sanctions. In still other cases it may be neutral toward a nuclear candidate's aspirations or may even selectively assist a state to acquire nuclear weapons. Its policies toward (1) a potential nuclear power that has not reached the point of deciding whether to produce nuclear weapons but has deliberately maintained the option may be different from its policies toward (2) a state that has definitely decided to acquire nuclear weapons or toward (3) a state that has already acquired them.

In each stage, the United States must balance its desire to retain the allegiance of an ally or to gain the favor of a nonaligned state against the dangers of extending American commitments, upsetting local balances of power, and creating additional nuclear triggers. In the last two stages, however, when the decision to acquire nuclear weapons has been made, the question will arise whether it is not wiser, on balance, to give material assistance—technological help, nuclear armament, or even nuclear warheads—to the nuclear candidate in order to enhance America's political influence and foster a safer nuclear force or, perhaps, a more stable local balance rather than to remain aloof from, or hostile toward, its nuclear program. The question will also arise whether it is not better to offer to a friendly fledgling nuclear state protection against counterpressures or against a possible preventive attack by a local adversary than to be as detached as possible from the policies and conflicts of that state. On the other hand, there may be circumstances in which it will be wise for the superpowers to conspicuously dissociate themselves from commitment to a small nuclear power or even to initiate preventive action, directly or by proxy, against another nuclear power and its nuclear facilities. The only valid generalization is that a single policy will not serve American national interests in every case when another state has a prospective, imminent, incipient, or established nuclear force.

The Soviet Union can be expected to follow a similarly diversified policy toward aspiring and new nuclear states, with the large exception that it will be quite unlikely to give nuclear weapons and warheads to any state. Occasionally American and Soviet policies toward potential nuclear states may coincide. For example, they might extend parallel guarantees of protection to a nuclear candidate or fledgling nuclear state against a Chinese nuclear attack, or they might tacitly agree not to intervene against each other's guarantees to, or sanctions against, a third state. But it seems quite unlikely that the prospective or actual spread of nuclear weapons to additional states will in itself create a general American-Soviet entente.

The general effect of the prospective or actual spread of nuclear weapons will be to accentuate existing conflicts rather than to create new ones. It may weaken some existing alignments but could strengthen others. In some cases the imminent or actual acquisition of nuclear weapons might lead to new formal military commitments and alliances, either with or against the nuclear candidate. In others it might hasten dealignment or promote realignments that are already in progress. But the prospect of nuclear proliferation will not in itself transform existing configurations of interest. Its most significant impact on alignments and alliances will occur where an ascending major nuclear power capable of threatening one or both of the superpowers poses a security threat to other states with the capacity to become nuclear counterpoises to that power. In the next ten or fifteen years this situation is most likely to develop in Asia in response to China's growing nuclear strength.

China's nuclear power will not only seem to threaten the security of Asian states; it will further challenge the credibility of America's military containment of China, just as Soviet nuclear advances called into question the willingness of the United States to oppose aggression in Europe. Against China, however, the United States will probably not have recourse to the measures with which it has reinforced the credibility of its commitment to Europe—an institutionalized alliance and American military presence on the mainland. At the same time, there are other states with vital interests in Asia that are threatened by China and that could become nuclear powers—Japan, India, and Australia. In addition the Soviet Union, in some ways, must be regarded as a nuclear counterpoise to China.

The question therefore arises whether the American interest in containing China may not be better served in the long run by encouraging, rather than trying to discourage, the creation of a nuclear multipolar balance of power in which American power is supplemented, and American commitments are somewhat relieved, by the power and commitments of others. This question is especially pertinent to American policy toward prospective Indian and Japanese nuclear forces. For, if neither Japan nor India assumes the role of a counterpoise to China and an active participant in Asian politics, the United States may be faced with the very difficult task of trying to organize deterrence in behalf of noncommunist states under exclusive American nuclear protection. That task would be all the more awkward if it had to be combined with the burden of trying to discourage Japanese and Indian nuclear forces by guarantees, rewards, and sanctions, especially if the Soviet Union were inclined to grant the assistance that the United States withheld.

On the other hand, neither China's nuclear force nor its foreign policy may look sufficiently menacing to challenge the adequacy of the United States nuclear umbrella. In that case, a combination of domestic, political, and economic-technical considerations might induce governments in the Asian-Pacific area to leave the management of the military balance to others, while pursuing as independent a course as possible, consistent with retaining the implicit or formal protection of the United States.

5. *Ballistic Missile Defense*

If nuclear weapons designed to destroy national societies with unprecedented efficiency have affected the role of alliances, one might reasonably expect weapons that could limit such destruction to affect alliances. In the next twenty years technological advances in ballistic missile defenses may be no less dramatic than advances in ballistic missiles have been in the past twenty years.

In 1966 the Soviet Union began deploying antiballistic missiles (ABM's) around Moscow and perhaps other cities. There was active speculation that it might also be contemplating a deployment along the so-called Tallinn Line in the northwest segment of Russia. This development and China's nuclear progress, which was perhaps more immediately decisive, led to an American decision in 1967 to install a "thin" deployment of ABM's.

Despite consternation in the United States that such a deployment might open up a whole new realm of nuclear competition, entailing economic and political costs without any net gain in security, it is not a foregone conclusion that the deployment will greatly accelerate or destabilize the American-Soviet arms race. The expense of ABM's, the many anti-ABM measures available to both sides, the inherent superiority of the strategic offense (considering the requirement of virtually perfect defense to prevent cata-

strophic strikes), the Soviet proclivity for producing only
modest amounts of a variety of weapons rather than using
their full capability for producing a particular weapon, and
the interest of both Washington and Moscow in preserving
an atmosphere of détente, seem likely to induce both sides to
confine deployments to moderate levels, intended to save
lives but not expected to nullify the deterrent effect of offensive missiles. Moreover, contrary to the case of ICBM's,
Soviet leaders have shown little or no inclination to exploit
an alleged superiority in ABM's to launch a more adventurous policy. Consequently, ABM's may be absorbed into the
over-all arms race gradually and with less shock than
ICBM's. If this holds true of ABM's, the same will probably
apply in the distant future to other ballistic missile defense
weapons such as space-borne weapons capable of intercept-
ing missiles during their ascent. Consequently, strategic
defensive weapons will have much less effect upon the balance of power, or the balance of resolve, between the superpowers than upon the positions of other states in relation to
the superpowers.

The most obvious politically significant effect of American
and Soviet ABM deployments will be to increase the disparity of power between them and the second-rank states,
including their nuclear allies. But this increased disparity
could have at least two different effects on alliances.

On the one hand, it might tend to limit the political
leverage that France and China could otherwise hope to ex-
tract from their offensive missile systems, since American
and Soviet ABM's will make the smaller forces of their respective deviant allies look less effective, even as weapons of
desperation. In this case, military bipolarity would be
strengthened and political polycentrism would be somewhat
weakened.

On the other hand, in reaction to the increased disparity
resulting from American and Soviet ABM's, second-rank nuclear allies and some nuclear-potential allies might simply

become more determined to pursue an independent military course for independent political purposes, since they would conclude that the superpowers are more interested in protecting their own inhabitants than those of their allies, and they would be determined not to be permanently priced out of the strategic nuclear market and forever condemned to inferior status. In NATO an American ABM deployment in response to a growing Soviet deployment may have the dual effect upon some allies—France and Germany most important among them—of making them feel more dependent on American nuclear protection, yet more dissatisfied with their dependence and more determined to escape it.

Other allies, however—allies who are not particularly dissatisfied with or anxious about their military dependence on the United States—may simply conclude that an American ABM system strengthens the American nuclear umbrella over them and therefore enhances the attractiveness of their alliance with the United States. The United Kingdom and Japan may fall into this category of reactions—especially Japan, since American ABM's will be far more effective against the infant Chinese nuclear force than against the Soviet force.

Nevertheless, one must doubt that any nuclear-potential state, Japan included, will be content simply to welcome American ABM's as a contribution to its security. In the long run, if the United States and the Soviet Union have decided that the utility of ABM's warrants spending the money to make them an integral element of their strategic weapons, any other nation that can afford them and feels that it is a potential target of nuclear strikes will probably want them, too. Nations like Japan, which are growing more conscious of status and searching for an acceptable way of demonstrating it, will find in ABM's a form of conspicuous military power that avoids the opprobrium that weapons of massive destruction have incurred.

American and Soviet ABM deployments will probably

have little direct effect on nonallies like India, which do not rely heavily on the nuclear protection of a superpower and are not concerned with countering a superpower's nuclear force. But these nations, too, may respond to the contagion of ABM deployments and find status and security to be adequate reasons for acquiring them. If so, only technical and economic obstacles may prevent them from carrying out national deployments.

So, estimation of the political effects of ABM's must take into account the prospect that states other than the superpowers will eventually seek or acquire them to protect their cities. They may acquire this protection by having the superpowers deploy ABM's to protect them, by direct ownership, or by joint control.

It seems likely that any state willing to pay for ABM's and/or have them deployed on its territory will want them under national control or else only under joint control that assures automatic use. For under these circumstances the protection of its own cities from incoming missiles is scarcely something that one state will leave to another to decide. Moreover, the very short reaction time required to make ABM's useful in Europe or Japan—a reaction time that precludes a joint political decision to pull the metaphorical ABM trigger—will reinforce the natural desire of every state to have exclusive control over the defense of its cities.[3] Then, too, the deployment of ABM's to protect another country will not provide the same sense of status to that

3. The only practicable joint control over ABM's would apply to turning the whole system "off" or "on" (depending, for example, on political warning of attack) and to verifying that ABM's were not adapted to ground-to-ground use. Even the control measures for these purposes might raise doubts about the automatic use of ABM's; yet, because neither the deliberate nor the inadvertent use of defensive weapons exploding far above the ground raises the same questions of national survival as the use of ground-to-ground missiles, the political problem of joint control should be easier.

country as if it were to deploy its own. For many years, however, very few states will be capable of producing their own ABM's, and the United States may not be willing to give ABM's as a gift. Consequently, the superpowers (or at least the United States), having deployed ABM's to protect themselves, will probably be under considerable pressure to extend such protection to their allies and to other states that feel threatened by a common adversary.

In the NATO area, unless great improvements in the cost-effectiveness of ABM's occur, the marginal utility of an ABM system, in the eyes of European governments, will probably not seem worth the expense of producing it, considering the density of the population and the vast number of Soviet IRBM's, not to mention bombers, that could attack Western Europe. Furthermore, the technical and economic feasibility of a useful system would require an integrated, centrally controlled system, at least for the continental countries; but for the reasons we have suggested it might be difficult for the countries involved to agree on an arrangement for joint control. Under these circumstances, if the United States deploys ABM's to protect itself without deploying them for the protection of Western Europe, it will probably alienate some of its allies and give credence to the Gaullist line. For if ABM's are good enough to save American lives, they will probably seem good enough to save European lives. Therefore, although American deployment of ABM's for the protection of its allies might be technically inadequate and politically galling, it will probably seem less objectionable than leaving Western Europe unprotected. And if the United States can deploy ABM's effectively at sea, it can avoid the political difficulties of deploying them on allied territory. Thus ABM's seem likely to strain relations between the United States and its allies, but American ABM policy can mitigate the strain.

For some states, receiving American or Soviet ABM's might one day become an important form of military assistance, especially if nuclear proliferation takes place and the ABM's provide a useful measure of protection against relatively small nuclear forces. Technical, financial, or material assistance to acquire ABM's could offer states that regard themselves as potential nuclear targets a form of protection—territorial self-defense—more compatible with a friendly superpower's interests than guarantees, nuclear sharing, or independent control of offensive nuclear weapons. (Of course, if the United States gives assistance to one state, it would be more difficult to refuse assistance to another, but there will not be so many candidates as to tax its resources.) Whether such assistance takes the form of deployments under the donor's control (again, seaborne ABM's would be advantageous) or of help to the recipient in making his own deployments, it is likely to entail some reciprocal assurances or compensations from the recipient. But, like other kinds of military assistance, ABM assistance would serve as a much less binding kind of commitment than alliance, and it might strengthen ties in an existing alliance.

Against China's nuclear force, ABM's may be both technically useful and economically feasible in the 1970's for India, Japan, and Australia to produce, especially if the United States were to give them economic and technical assistance. In any case, these countries may want to buy American ABM's for their own use. For nuclear-potential states like Japan and India—where domestic opposition to a nuclear program springs from a special aversion to nuclear weapons and the fear of making the country more vulnerable to attack—the acquisition of ABM's may provide an attractive alternative to producing an offensive nuclear force, since weapons that promise to save lives in one's own nation (even though they use nuclear warheads) will enhance national security and status without arousing the kind of opposition caused by weapons that would destroy millions of enemy lives and provoke comparable retaliatory damage. The superpowers are also likely to view ABM's as an attractive alternative to nuclear proliferation, since they might divert sentiment for proliferation without posing the threat of independent nuclear action inherent in an ally's possession of offensive nuclear weapons.

Consequently, under some conditions the United States, and perhaps even the Soviet Union, may want to assist vulnerable nuclear-potential states in acquiring ABM's by gift or otherwise as an alternative to either extending nuclear guarantees or trying to discourage offensive nuclear missile programs by such discriminatory means as withholding technical and financial assistance or sponsoring nonproliferation agreements. If the dispersion of ABM's did serve this purpose, it would tend to offset the pressure for additional United States commitments and to strengthen existing commitments.

However, the United States would have to weigh this consideration against the prospect that a nuclear-potential state's acquisition of ABM's might eventually encourage and facilitate that state's acquisition of offensive nuclear weapons. The acquisition of ABM's raises this prospect for several reasons: it would tend to diminish the opprobrium attached to all kinds of nuclear weapons and would provide valuable technical experience for producing ground-to-ground missiles; the interdependence of offensive and defensive weapons in the strategic nuclear equation would make it seem illogical to possess one without the other; and proliferation of ABM's might upset local military balances and stimulate arms races in other kinds of nuclear weapons.

Because of the risk that ABM's would lead to IRBM's and ICBM's, Communist China's deployment of ABM's might be a more effective discouragement to a Japanese or Indian offensive nuclear program than the acquisition of ABM's by these countries. And Chinese ABM's would not call into question America's deterrent umbrella over its allies because they would be ineffective against the very much larger and more advanced American striking force. But it is as unlikely that China will acquire ABM's without leading her major potential adversaries to acquire them or to seek the protection of American ABM's as that the Soviet Union could deploy ABM's without causing an American deployment. The political obstacles to the proliferation of ABM's are far weaker than obstacles to the proliferation of offensive nuclear weapons. It probably follows that, once both the United States and the Soviet Union integrate a conspicuous number of ABM's into their armed forces, it will be difficult for either (but especially for the United States) to turn down requests for ABM protection or assistance from allies and, to a lesser extent, from nonallies with a nuclear potential, without jeopardizing alliances and alignments.

But all conjectures about the effects of ABM's on the role of alliances in United States policy are quite fallible. In the first place, the psychological and political reactions to ABM's will depend very much on the particular circumstances in which one state or another acquires and deploys them, the explicit and implicit rationale underlying their acquisition or deployment, future technological changes in strategic offensive and defensive weapons, and many other unpredictable factors. In the second place, the correlation between whatever psychological and political reactions to ABM's may occur and the views of nations and governments about the utility or disutility of alliances and other commitments is quite uncertain, since there are so many other kinds of considerations that will have at least as much bearing upon such views. At this point it looks as though Soviet and American deployments of ABM's will have less impact upon alliances outside Europe than either advancements in airlift and sealift or the prospective and actual spread of offensive nuclear weapons, but they seem likely to have more impact on relations between the United States and its allies in NATO. Yet where so much depends on emotional and popular reactions and upon the circumstances, procedures, and official justifications of ABM policies in the United States and the Soviet Union, such estimates are highly conditional.

6. *The Future of Alliances*

I have examined major functions and determinants of alliances and their effects on the role of alliances as the international political environment has changed. In this final chapter, I have speculated about future changes in the international environment, including technological changes. Such speculation is bound to be too imprecise and contingent to lead to confident predictions about the future of alliances, but it can serve as a kind of checklist of factors pertinent to the unpredictable specific events and circumstances that may arise.

Here I shall briefly suggest the relevance of this analysis to the aspect of the future of alliances that was initially singled out as being particularly significant for American policy—the problem of preponderance. More precisely, though less simply, this is the problem of limiting American commitments to those in which the United States can effectively protect its interests with a level of effort and involvement that the political will and genius of the nation can sustain.

The most general observation one can safely make is that the period in which alliances were largely a vehicle for the extension of American military deterrence, and in which the dominant American role in its alliances was defined and determined by the military necessities of containment, has passed and is not likely to be repeated. This is not because the military containment of the Soviet Union and China will cease to be an important concern but, rather, because the organization of containment will be politically more complicated, and less readily dominated by the American view of military necessities, than it was during the first decade of NATO and while alliances were being extended beyond Europe after the Korean War. Moreover, compared with deterrence, a variety of political functions, including the restraint of allies, will be more important than they were in those formative periods.

Alliances will remain an integral part of international

politics among sovereign states having interdependent interests, interacting policies, and the military power to support
them. Although the postwar alliances of the United States
are products of the cold war, alliances would play a significant role in American foreign policy even if the cold war
had ended. But this analysis suggests that there have been
some significant changes in United States alliance policy,
and that more changes will occur as alliances are adapted to
new international developments. It also suggests that the
role of other kinds of military commitments will continue to
increase, leaving alliances as the hard core of a diversified
aggregation of commitments.

It is not likely that American commitments to use force
will diminish in geographical extent. On the contrary, they
may increase, at least in Asia. Nonetheless, political circumstances may permit, if not compel, a more modest scale of
commitment. That is, the obligations and responsibilities
entailed in various commitments may become more limited
and flexible. This trend would be reflected in the avoidance
of far-reaching new alliance commitments, a relatively larger
role for commitments other than alliances, and the diminished urgency of the external security functions of existing
alliances.

This situation would be favorable from the standpoint of
those Americans who long to limit the entanglements of the
United States. Yet it would carry its own frustrations, perhaps to such an extent as to call into question the nation's
will to maintain existing commitments. In NATO the
United States can expect to encounter a growing disproportion between the extent of its military responsibilities and
the extent of its control of alliance policy. For the changing
political environment in Europe will encourage independent activity on the part of allies without diminishing American preponderance in the management of the military balance vis-à-vis Russia. Moreover, the problem of maintaining
allied cohesion will be complicated by increasingly absorb-

ing problems of interallied relations and East-West politics, on which there is less of a consensus than on the requirements of military security.

In adjusting to this situation the United States probably cannot go much further by extending allied participation in military control or "crisis management." Nor does the formula for closing the gap between responsibilities and control lie in strengthening military and political "integration." Rather, the United States must further differentiate its relations with various allies as particular circumstances dictate, while trying to preserve a close working collaboration, especially with West Germany. America's political energies will be expended in orchestrating its special relationships with allies and accommodating their divergent political positions in a reasonably harmonious coalition rather than in trying to secure detailed adherence to American military and diplomatic policies, endorsed by united NATO positions.

In this political task the United States will be dealing with allies that are much more nearly its equal in political influence than in military power, especially if several of the European allies form a special coalition for diplomatic and military co-operation. This will complicate America's role in the alliance. On the other hand, within a stable military balance it should also permit a less intensive involvement and less exclusive responsibility. The question is whether the nation will be willing, over the long run, to maintain even a reduced burden of responsibility without having the compelling incentives for a united deterrent alliance that inspired the organization of NATO in an earlier and simpler period.

Trends in overseas transport technology could facilitate the adjustment of the United States to more diversified, flexible, and permissive relationships in NATO by reducing its dependence on elaborate, land-bound infrastructure, although some highly specialized military requirements, as in air defense, may demand closer technical integration. Yet as long as a Western European military union is infeasible, psychological and political considerations will dictate the advisability of maintaining United States forces in Europe.

Outside Europe there may be no significant extension of American commitments by alliances. If there is such an extension, the alliances will entail a much more limited scale of obligation than in Europe, or, for that matter, than in SEATO and the alliance with Japan—with the possible exception of a postwar alliance with South Vietnam, comparable to those with the South Koreans and the Chinese on Taiwan. The most likely but still doubtful scene of such an extension is in Asia, where, in a decade or so, new alliances might consolidate a multipolar balance of power among major military powers. But if such a multipolar balance emerges, the United States will be one power among several in a network of guarantees rather than the hegemonial leader of a coalition. If Japan were an active participant in such a balance—and that is virtually a precondition for the emergence of a multipolar structure of power—it would scarcely remain under the tutelage of the United States, and its alliance with the United States probably would have to be revised accordingly. The resulting pattern of alliances would be more like the network that Bismarck established, in an effort to order Europe's international politics after the Franco-Prussian War, than like the bipolar confrontation of coalitions before World War I and after World War II. As in Europe, this more pluralistic and loosely knit network of political relations would give the United States a better opportunity to limit the scale of its obligations and increase its freedom of action than if it were the exclusive container of China; but, even more than in Europe, it would also complicate the government's policy problems and offer the nation a less compelling rationale for military commitments than existed in the aftermath of the Korean War.

Again, advances in the mobility of American forces will facilitate America's technical adjustment to such a future pattern of alliances by increasing the range, speed, and volume of military transport and supply, and by making United States forces less dependent on land bases and infrastructure. However, physical mobility may not obviate the occasional need for short-term deployments of American forces on land. United States policies toward additional independent nuclear forces and ballistic missile defenses will have to be flexible and diversified in order to adjust to the increasingly complicated structure of power and pattern of conflict outside Europe.

Among the less-developed countries, any extension of American commitments will almost surely take place chiefly by means other than alliances. In some respects political developments make an extension of American commitments more feasible than before. Notably, some political conditions that seemed to favor nonalignment have changed. Nonalignment, as a tactic to take advantage of superpower competition while avoiding entanglement in it, has been deprived of some of its value for the new states by the superpowers' diminished competition in the Third World, the onset of détente, and the emergence of political polycentrism and of a more complicated pattern of global politics. The subjective appeal of nonalignment, along with that of anticolonialism and anti-Westernism, has declined, and the immediate problems of building states and nations—the problems of internal and external security—have become more relevant to the interests of new countries. In a number of states new regimes that are more interested in coping with fundamental tasks of economic and political survival than in manipulating the symbols of personal and national status have facilitated mutually useful relations with great powers. The intensification of local national conflicts has somewhat increased the incentives of small states to seek military support from extraregional states.

Despite these trends, however, the political and military factors limiting the alliance capability of the less-developed countries are likely to persist. Few of these states will have the military power, the internal strength and stability, or the well-established external interests related to military power to enable them to engage in military alliances. Both international and internal politics will be too fluid and unpredictable to be consolidated and regularized through alliances. The foreign policies of the small and poor states will be too inchoate and unreliable to attract the great powers to alliances.

The superpowers, confronted by the limited pay-offs and maximum hazards of backing client states, will want to insulate themselves further from the turmoil of the Third World. Consequently, instead of the superpowers' seeking allies and the small, poor states' resisting alliance, the situation may be reversed. Military technology will make it easier for weak states in the Third World to accept alliance with a great power because of the diminished need for its presence in their countries, but weak states will also have less to offer to advanced military states because of the diminished value of bases and facilities. Although the accentuation of local conflicts in the Third World may give the weak states new incentives to seek the protection and support of alliance with a great power, the incentives for the great powers are not commensurate; and the disincentives for the superpowers will grow if local conflicts become increasingly dissociated from ideological issues and the global contest.

To some extent the superpowers and, possibly, the once-great powers may want alliances in the Third World in order to extend their influence and status and to keep weak states from making alliances with competitors in a contest with extraregional powers for regional primacy. In some cases the United States may form alliances to preserve the minimum conditions of international order. For the sake of order the United States might wish to form alliances with small states to protect them from local imperialism and subversion or to promote the regional military-political core of a subsystem. But for any of these motives—allegiance or control, status or order—alliances, compared to other means of influence, are likely to be too conspicuous, inflexible, and entangling to be attractive instruments of policy for extraregional powers. Unless well-developed regional systems should crystallize around core states with stable regimes, even short-term alliances of the most limited sort will be relatively clumsy instruments of policy compared to military assistance agreements, informal assurances, unilateral declarations of intent, and the like. But there may be one important exception to this generalization—alliances between former colonies and their metropoles, where special cultural and political affinities coincide with the economic and status interests of the metropole.

Ideally, yet within the realm of possibility, America's interest in a reasonably orderly international environment, imposing tolerable demands on American power, would be served best if the states in the Third World would structure their relations in local balances of power by means of stable alliances among themselves. For the consolidation of local systems by this means might bring latent conflicts among the lesser states into the open without generating new ones and might serve to contain and adjust them in a regular fashion. It would also enable weak states to relate to major extraregional powers on mutually advantageous terms in which the disparity of power would be less embarrassing to the former and less burdensome to the latter. In fact, however, the same military and political conditions that limit the capability of the less-developed countries to form alliances with great powers will impede their forming them with each other. And even if the states of Africa, the Middle East, and Southeast Asia were to impress order upon their political relations through systems of alliances, the prospect of stable balances of power—which seem, historically, to depend on a rare conjunction of favorable circumstances—would be slight. Unfortunately, one precondition of such balances of power may be a long period of disorder and violence accompanying a sporadic process of building nations and international systems, with alliances emerging from actual and imminent warfare before they can reflect more permanent alignments of vital interests.

Meanwhile, the nearest thing to indigenous and autonomous systems of international order in the Third World will be various regional or continental associations, unions, or concerts, like the Organization of African Unity or the Asian and Pacific Council. A few of these organizations (like the Association of Southeast Asian Nations) may be incipient alliances responding to a genuine consensus of security interests in opposition to a specific security threat. But most of them are cryptoalliances, which try to mute or conceal the actual military and political conflicts and alignments among their members and tend to become engrossed with the rhetoric and symbols of collaboration. Self-consciously avoiding territorial questions and the issues of security and power, they prefer to concentrate on broader economic, cultural, and political matters upon which they can agree more readily. Nevertheless, these associations could be important schools of political education. If they survive the intensification and crystallization of local power politics, they may be important transitional devices on the road to more regularized and responsible participation in international politics. By providing an element of cohesion and a sense of collective strength, they may make *de facto* alignments with extraregional powers more acceptable to weak states and enable great powers to extend military and economic assistance without becoming too involved in critical local issues. Some of them may even nurture the seeds of indigenous alliances.

When one surveys all these trends, the functions of American alliances in the future seem considerably more diversified, yet more limited, than in the network of regional multilateral and local bilateral deterrent alliances that the United States government evidently looked forward to making the foundation of its foreign policy after the Korean War. American military commitments of all kinds are likely to persist and even multiply in the absence of Soviet and Chinese retrenchment or the emergence of important new counterpoises in the world balance of power. But the variety, limited scope, diverse objectives, and, in many cases, ambiguous and esoteric nature of commitments other than alliances will deprive them of the appeal, as a means of reconciling the United States to its global role, that American alliances used to have and were expected to have in the future. They will fail to appeal, as they did in the period of alliance-building, to America's original ideal of constructing a world order—of building an institutionalized system of interdependent relationships that transcend old-fashioned nationalism and deter a united global enemy dedicated to a competing system of world order. These other commitments, in their aggregate function, are more comparable to the instrumentalities of empire, but they do not provide the satisfactions of true empire to justify them.

America's adjustment to the change of expectations and role that the future of alliances will require is part of its general problem of adjusting to the more complex pattern of international politics that is now emerging. The most serious question about the nation's ability to make this adjustment concerns its political will and the wisdom of its leaders, not its physical capacity.

Index